Metric & Ir

Air Fryer UK Recipes

Ultimate UK Cookbook

Home Chef Books

Compatible with all air fryers

We acknowledge that there are various makes and models of air fryers available. Still, our recipes are compatible with any air fryer with an air fryer setting, including the new Ninja Woodfire Outdoor Grill. Look out for our book "The Woodfire Way".

Some air fryers are air fry only, which is excellent too. In some instances, you may need to make slight adjustments to your settings, depending on the power and model of your air fryer. However, a little experimentation should produce perfect dishes. To prepare these dishes, you won't need to grill, bake, roast, or do anything other than air fry. Follow instructions and adjust the temperature and time on your air fryer as needed.

Copyright 2023©homechefbooks. This book is intended to provide information concerning the topic covered. All rights are reserved, and no reproduction, duplicating or transmitting any part of this book is permitted without the author's consent. Information herein is offered for informational purposes only.

Metric and Imperial Measurements

This publication's use of metric and imperial units of measurement means more than appealing to a broad readership. In the UK, many still use both units of measurement daily. So you can still visit many UK shops, such as a butcher, and ask for just over two pounds of steak or a kilogram, and you will not be given a confused look. However, you will likely get a funny look if you ask for a beer in a pub using metric.

Imperial measurements appear to be embedded in British culture. Miles are the most prominent on a vehicle's speedometer. Road signs are in miles, not kilometres. We talk about people's height in feet, more often than centimetres, but we buy pre-packed food items in grams and kilograms.

Long ago, 1 foot measured a person's foot, or thereabouts; an inch was a finger's width. A yard was from nose to thumb. The Roman Empire defined the mile as one thousand paces. Even today, horses are still measured in hands.

The decimal-based metric system using units of 10s was taken up just a few hundred years ago. It was said to be a system based on logic or the surroundings. The distance between the North Pole and the equator was used to create a metre, seen as one ten-millionth of that distance. One cubic centimetre's volume of water was a millilitre, equalling one gram. The UK's imperial weights and measures system was officially changed to European metric units in 1968. However, it still has some way to go before imperial measurements are gone, if at all.

There are still a few holdouts, such as in the USA, where the imperial system is still used. The metric system is unlikely to be fully integrated with the imperial or replace it. It is down to time, money, and a much stronger rejection of the metric system in the USA than in the UK and the UK's closer ties to the rest of Europe. During the industrial revolution, machines in the USA were set up using imperial units, and people were trained to use those units.

The UK once had several different gallon measurements, so the USA took on the Queen Anne Wine Gallon, 231 cubic inches, as opposed to the Elizabethan gallon of 282 cubic inches. With the UK's metric system's introduction, the gallon changed to about 277 cubic inches or about 4.55 litres. The USA gallon is 231 cubic inches or 3.78 litres, equivalent to 4 USA quarts.

It can all get a little confusing for some. Still, when it comes to cooking, it needn't be, and thankfully, even for sizeable family meal purposes, we often don't need to be so exact that we compare UK and USA imperial units. For example, when scooping two cups of flour, we rarely care if one cup is more compact. Over 90% of the world's population has been metricised, but we're all together regarding our love of food. In this publication, we have included the following units of measure to cater for all in the UK.

Cup, teaspoon (**tsp**), tablespoon (**tbsp**), pound (**lb**), ounce (**oz**), gram (**g**), kilogram (**kg**), millilitre (**ml**), litre (**l**), inch, millimetre (**mm**) and centimetre (**cm**). Fahrenheit (**F**) was named after the scientist Daniel Gabriel Fahrenheit from Poland, and Celsius (**C**) was named after the Swedish astronomer Anders Celsius.

A Selection of Popular Foods and Cooking Times

Meats	Temperature	Cooking Time
Bacon	350F/180C	8-12
Burgers (1/4lb 114g)	350F/180C	8-12
Chicken (3.5lb 1.6kg)	350F/180C	45-60
Chicken Breasts	350F/180C	8-12
Chicken Drumsticks	400F/200C	15
Chicken Thighs	400F/200C	10-16
Chicken Breast Strips	350F/180C	8-12
Chicken Wings	350F/180C	14-16
Fillet Steak (8oz 225g)	400F/200C	18
Lamb Chops	400F/200C	8-12
Meatballs	400F/200C	5-8
Pork Chops	400F/200C	15
Pork Loin (Whole)	360F/185C	18-21
Rack of Lamb	375F/190C	22
Ribeye Steak	400F/200C	12
Pork Ribs	400F/200C	10-15
Silverside	400F/200C	10-15
Sausages	400F/200C	15
Sirloin Steak	390F/195C	9-14
Tenderloin	365F/185C	15

Vegetables	Temperature	Cooking Time
Asparagus	400F/200C	5-7
Beetroot	400F/200C	40
Broccoli Florets	400F/200C	6
Brussels Sprouts (Halves)	380F/195C	15
Carrots Sliced	360F/185C	15
Cauliflower Florets	400F/200C	12-15
Corn on the Cob	390F/195C	8
Aubergine slices	400F/200C	15
Green Beans	400F/200C	6-8
Mushrooms	400F/200C	5
Onions	400F/200C	10
Peppers (Bell)	380F/195C	10
Pepper Chunks (Bell)	380F/195C	8
Potato		
Baby	400F/200C	15
Wedges	400F/200C	15
Diced	400F/200C	12
Whole	400F/200C	45
Butternut Squash Chunks	400F/200C	2
Sweet Potatoes	380F/195C	30-35
Cherry Tomatoes	400F/200C	5
Courgettes	400F/200C	12

Frozen Food	Temperature	Cooking Time
Cheese Sticks	390F/195C	10
Chicken Nuggets	390F/195C	10
Fish Fillets	390F/195C	10
Fish Fingers	390F/195C	15
Chips (Thick)	400F/200C	20
French Fries (Thin)	400F/200C	15
Spring Rolls	400F/200C	15-20

Seafood	Temperature	Cooking Time
Calamari	400F/200C	6
Fish Fillets	400F/200C	10-12
Salmon Fillets	350F/180C	8-12
Scallops	400F/200C	6-8
Prawns	350F/180C	6-8
Tuna Steak	400F/200C	8-12

Snacks and Desserts	Temperature	Cooking Time
Baked Apples	400F/200C	15
Banana Bread	360F/185C	25
Brownies	325F/170C	30
Cake (Whole)	350F/180C	20-25
Biscuits	300F/150C	10
Muffins (Large)	375F/190C	15-20
Cupcakes	360F/185C	15
Pastries	325F/170C	10-12
Pizza for One	400F/200C	10-15
Quiche (Whole)	360F/185C	25-30

To make it easier to manage the settings on your air fryer, temperatures are rounded to approximate whole numbers. However, it's important to note that cooking times are also approximate and may vary depending on the texture and amount of food and the air fryer's model and make.

You should check on the food regularly when you cook it for the first time in your air fryer to ensure it's cooked to your liking. You may need to adjust the cooking times, ingredients, weights, and measurements to suit your preferences.

Conversion Chart

Spoon, Cups & Liquids

1/4 tsp	1.25ml
1/2 tsp	2.5ml
1 tsp	5 ml
1 tbsp	15 ml
1/4 cup	60 ml
1/3 cup	80 ml
1/2 cup	125 ml
1 cup	250 ml

Dry Measurements

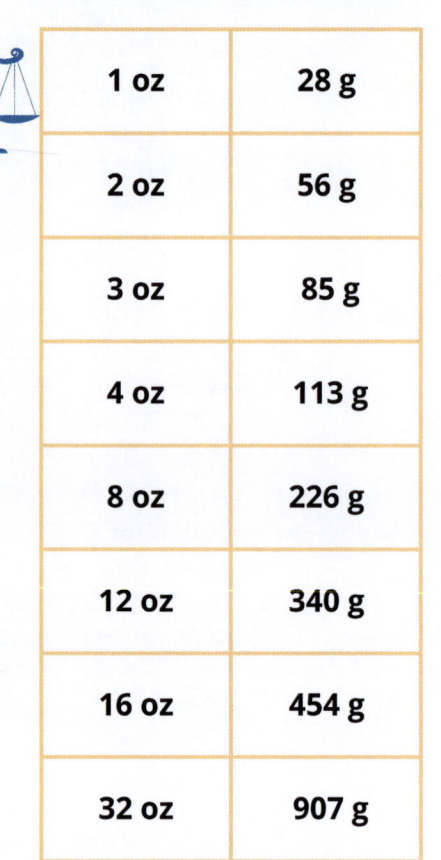

1 oz	28 g
2 oz	56 g
3 oz	85 g
4 oz	113 g
8 oz	226 g
12 oz	340 g
16 oz	454 g
32 oz	907 g

Temperatures

275 f	140 c
300 f	150 c
325 f	170 c
350 f	180 c
375 f	190 c
400 f	200 c
425 f	220 c
450 f	230 c

Popular Ingredients

1 Cup Flour	120 g
1 Cup Butter	127 g
1 Cup White Sugar	200 g
1 Cup Brown Sugar	220 g

To simplify things, the weights and measures provided are approximate and rounded off to remove decimals. Additionally, it is important to note that there may be ingredient variations due to differences in manufacturing or suppliers.

Which Air Fry?

Air fryers are excellent kitchen gadgets, enabling you to prepare tasty and healthier versions of your favourite fried foods quickly and easily. Instead of immersing the food in oil, an air fryer employs hot air to cook the food.

This method results in a crispy and crunchy texture without the need for excess fat and calories. Furthermore, air fryers usually consume less energy than conventional cooking methods, making them an efficient and cost-effective option. An air fryer can cook various dishes, from classic French fries to fried fish, chicken, and vegetables.

What Size?

The appropriate size of the air fryer is contingent upon the quantity of food you intend to cook in it. For instance, if you plan on cooking for a small family of one or two people, a smaller air fryer that can hold 1-2 litres should suffice. However, if you plan to prepare meals for a larger family or entertain guests, a larger air fryer between 5.8-7.6, litres may be more appropriate. Since the air fryer's size determines the amount of food you can cook at once, it is crucial to assess how you plan to use it before purchasing.

How To Clean?

Cleaning an air fryer is a straightforward process that can be accomplished in a few easy steps. To begin, turn off and unplug the air fryer and remove any remaining food particles or debris from the basket. Subsequently, wipe down the basket, lid, and external parts of the fryer with a damp cloth. If necessary, a mild detergent can eliminate any stubborn residue. Once all surfaces are clean, use a dry cloth to dry the fryer. Finally, reassemble the air fryer and plug it in to use.

Safety?

- Always read the instruction manual for your air fryer before using it for the first time.
- Place the air fryer on a flat, stable surface, away from flammable materials.
- Refrain from overfilling the basket.
- Wear oven mitts when handling hot air fryer parts.
- Keep the air fryer away from children and pets.
- Unplug the air fryer when not in use.
- Check the air fryer's cords and plugs for any signs of damage.
- Use the proper amount and type of cooking oil recommended by the manufacturer.
- Never leave the air fryer unattended while it is in use.
- Look over the air fryer and its location for potential problems before each use.

Interesting Air Fryer Points

Safe To Use

Microwave ovens are known for their convenience and speed, but unlike microwaves, air fryers do not emit radiation during cooking or make food radioactive. Instead, they function by heating food through the vibration of water molecules, which results in hot food. On the other hand, air fryers use radiation to generate heat, which quickly circulates within the fryer, resulting in crispy food rather than soggy food. This contrasts with microwaved pies or Cornish pasties, which typically do not come out crispy.

Reduced Harmful Compounds

When certain foods are cooked at high temperatures using any cooking method, they can produce harmful compounds such as acrylamide, heterocyclic amines, and polycyclic aromatic hydrocarbons. Consumption of these compounds can pose a health risk to humans and, in some rare cases, may even lead to cancer. Therefore, it is worth noting that cooking any food at high temperatures using any cooking method can form these harmful compounds.

- While meat is a significant contributor, other foods cooked at high heat can also create these compounds. According to research, air-frying has been found to potentially decrease the level of acrylamide by as much as 90%.

- Studies have indicated that air frying can reduce the presence of potentially cancer-causing compounds like heterocyclic amines. Nevertheless, as the duration and temperature of cooking increase, so does the likelihood of these compounds forming.

- The main idea is that using an air fryer to cook food quickly at high temperatures may be a healthier option than using a conventional oven and cooking for extended periods. However, it is essential to be mindful of the convenience of air fryers, as they could increase cooking frequency. Therefore, it is best to limit daily use.

Energy Saving

Although air fryers consume less energy than traditional cooking methods, some individuals utilise them more frequently throughout the day, potentially resulting in greater energy consumption. To determine the kWh (kilowatt hours) consumed in a day, one can multiply the wattage of a small air fryer (e.g., 1000 watts) by the number of hours it has been in use. For instance, if the air fryer has been in use for 3 hours, the total wattage would be 3000, which would be divided by 1000, resulting in 3 kWh.

While this straightforward calculation can be performed mentally, it can be advantageous for appliances with varying wattages. Afterwards, the kWh consumed can be compared to what would have been used if traditional kitchen appliances, such as an oven, were used to determine energy savings. However, despite the potential savings, air frying has been scientifically proven to be a healthy cooking method.

Weight Loss

Air fryers are kitchen appliances that utilise hot air for cooking food. They are commonly marketed as a healthier alternative to traditional deep frying due to their lower requirement of cooking oil. As a result, the calorie and fat content of food cooked in an air fryer may be reduced.

Nevertheless, it should be kept in mind that the health benefits of air fryers depend on the ingredients and cooking techniques employed. For example, cooking processed frozen foods containing high levels of salt, sugar, and artificial additives may not result in a healthy outcome, unlike using an air fryer for cooking fresh vegetables.

Overall, air fryers are functional appliances for preparing healthy meals at home. Nevertheless, it is crucial to bear in mind that the healthfulness of the resulting food will be significantly influenced by the ingredients and cooking methods employed.

Food Rotation

When using a microwave or conventional oven, we can usually rely on the timer to indicate when the food is ready. However, when using an air fryer, it's crucial to periodically check and flip the food during cooking to ensure even hot air circulation. This will help achieve evenly cooked results.

Handy Air Fryer Accessories

Ovenproof Pans and Bowls

Any accessory must withstand high heat for an air fryer, meaning ovenproof items will work well. With so many brands and models on the market, it's important to research to determine the most suitable for your requirements.

When selecting a pan or bowl, choosing one made of durable, heat-resistant materials like Pyrex, stainless steel, or ceramic-coated aluminium is best. Furthermore, ensure that the pan size is appropriate for your air fryer, allowing the hot air to circulate freely.

Measuring Spoons and Cups

Sometimes, time and convenience are of the essence, so measuring spoons and cups can be extremely handy.

Measuring spoons are small utensils used for measuring small quantities of liquid or dry ingredients for cooking or baking. They can come in a set of various sizes, usually including a teaspoon (tsp), tablespoon (tbsp), and sometimes a 1/4 or 1/2 teaspoon (1/4 tsp or 1/2 tsp) and 1/4 or 1/2 tablespoon (1/4 tbsp or 1/2 tbsp). They are usually made of metal, plastic or a combination of both and are designed to accurately measure small amounts of ingredients.

Kitchen measuring cups measure the volume of liquid or dry ingredients when cooking or baking. They typically come in a set that includes cups of various sizes, such as 1 cup, 1/2 cup, 1/3 cup, and 1/4 cup. They can be made of plastic, stainless steel, or glass. Some measuring cups have markings on the side, allowing for more precise measurements. Measuring spoons and cups are essential tools for any home chef.

Air Fryer Trivet Rack

An air fryer trivet rack is a metal stand positioned at the bottom of the appliance to lift food off the base and away from other layers, promoting proper air circulation and preventing the food from sticking. In the absence of a rack, cooking food in a single layer is recommended to avoid clumping and uneven cooking. You can cook an additional layer of food using a trivet rack.

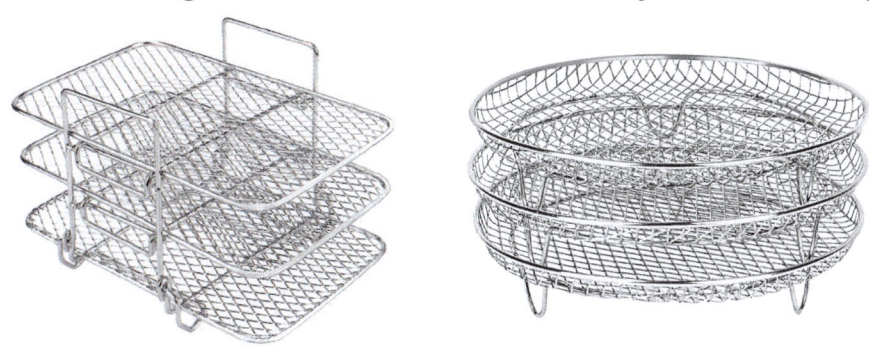

Springform or Removable Base

A springform or false-bottom tray/pan is a baking pan with detachable sides. It enables the safe and effortless release of delicate desserts, like cheesecake, without ruining their crust or sides. The sides of the pan are secured by a spring-lock mechanism, which can be opened by pressing a button or turning a knob. While round-shaped springform pans are common, they can also be found in square or rectangular shapes, and they're usually crafted from metal and come in multiple sizes.

Oven Mitts

Protective gloves or fingerless sleeves can help with transporting hot cookware to and from the air fryer. They are typically constructed from materials that can withstand high temperatures, such as silicone, neoprene, or cotton batting, and are designed to safeguard the hands and wrists from burns.

Batter Splatter

A common misconception is that wet batter cannot be used in an air fryer due to the risk of splattering caused by the hot circulating air. However, you can use a few tricks to help prevent this issue. If you're struggling with consistency in wet batter recipes, try implementing these tips. You might even find it enjoyable to experiment with stopping the batter splatter.

Before attempting anything else, it's worth noting that while some air fryers may struggle to keep the batter attached to the food, not all do. If your air fryer is prone to removing the batter before it sets, consider lowering the temperature slightly while increasing the cooking time. Cooking at a lower temperature for extended periods can often work wonders. Additionally, to minimise the risk of batter splatter, attach a sheet of tin foil to the top of a rack above the food to prevent the full force of the heated air from directly hitting the food.

Thicker Batter. Step One: Prepare the thickest, most viscous batter possible for the recipe. If the batter appears too thin, add some flour and mix well until you reach the desired consistency. With time and practice, you'll get the hang of using batter in your air fryer and enjoy the process. To apply the batter to the food, place the food in the batter in a container and refrigerate for 30 minutes. Occasionally shaking the container will help the batter penetrate the food's crevices.

Step Two: Remove each food item from the container and, while the batter is still thick and sticky, gently coat them with dry plain flour by rolling or flipping them. Afterwards, lightly spray each piece with cooking, vegetable, or olive oil. Then, place the food items back into the fridge on a plate or dish until ready to use them. It's a good idea to prepare battered food items well in advance of the meal.

Step Three: Once prepared, put the food that has been battered, floured, and oiled, into the air fryer basket and follow the recipe's cooking instructions. If time permits, lower the temperature and cook for a bit longer until the food reaches the desired appearance and level of doneness as indicated in the recipe.

My Notes and Recipes

My Notes and Recipes

My Notes and Recipes

My Notes and Recipes

My Notes and Recipes

Recipes

- Snacks and Starters
- Vegetable and Sides
- Fish and Seafood
- Chicken and Poultry
- Desserts
- Breakfast
- Pork, Beef, and Lamb
- Soups, Stews, Curries

#	Recipe	Page
1	Cheese Toastie	1
2	Crumpets	1
3	Devilled Eggs	2
4	Eggy Bread	2
5	Full English Breakfast	3
6	Hard Boiled Eggs	3
7	No Mess Egg On Toast	4
8	Poached Eggs	4
9	Scrapple	5
10	Welsh Rarebit	5
11	Bacon Wrapped Pineapple	6
12	Bagels	6
13	Banana Chips	7
14	Battered Cheese Curds	7
15	Battered Crab Sticks	8
16	Blooming Onion	8
17	Breaded Cheese Sticks	9
18	Carrot Chips	9
19	Cauliflower Bites	10
20	Cheese Stuffed Burger	10
21	Chicken Wings	11
22	Cornish Pasty	11
23	Crispy Chickpeas	12
24	Crispy Pizza	12
25	Flowered Cauliflower	13
26	Fried Pickles	13
27	Grilled Cheese In Milk	14
28	Macaroni Cheese	14
29	Meatball Roll	15
30	Nut Loaf	15
31	Onion Rings	16
32	Pigs In Blankets	16
33	Popcorn Chicken	17
34	Potato Peel Crisps	17
35	Reuben Sandwich	18
36	Salt & Pepper Chips	18
37	Sausage Rolls	19
38	Scotch Eggs	19
39	Spicy Roast Peanuts	20
40	Sweet Potato Crisps	20
41	Thin Cut Fries	21
42	Thin Kale Chips	21
43	*Chicken Tikka Masala*	22
44	*White Rice*	22
45	Cock-A-Leekie Soup	23
46	Cullen Skink	23
47	Irish Stew	24
48	Lancashire Hot Pot	24
49	Scouse	25
50	Welsh Cawl	25
51	Baked Cod	26
52	Baked Monkfish	26
53	Baked Salmon	27
54	Baked Squid	27
55	Breaded Scampi	28
56	Coconut Prawns	28
57	Fish Cakes	29
58	Fish Fingers	29
59	Mussels In Cream Sauce	30
60	Chicken Cutlets	30
61	Chicken Goujons	31
62	Chicken Honey Mustard	31
63	Chicken Rissoles	32
64	Chicken Thighs	32
65	Coronation Chicken	33
66	Crispy Chicken Fillets	33
67	Fried Chicken Breasts	34
68	Hunters Chicken	34
69	Parmo	35
70	*Bechamel Sauce*	35
71	Peri Peri Chicken	36
72	*Peri Peri Sauce*	36
73	Stuffed Chicken & Bacon	37
74	Whole Roast Chicken	37
75	Turkey Crown	38
76	BBQ Ribs	38
77	Beef Wellington	39
78	Boneless Welsh Lamb	39
79	Cottage Pie	40
80	Crispy Pork Belly	40

Recipes

- Snacks and Starters
- Vegetable and Sides
- Fish and Seafood
- Chicken and Poultry
- Desserts
- Breakfast
- Pork, Beef, and Lamb
- Soups, Stews, Curries

#	Recipe	Page	#	Recipe	Page
81	Faggots In Gravy	41	121	Hasselback Potatoes	61
82	Gammon Joint	41	122	Marmite Roast Potatoes	61
83	Lamb Chops	42	123	Mushrooms & Stilton	62
84	Lamb Shanks	42	124	Potato Balls	62
85	Meat & Potato Pie	43	125	Potato Cakes	63
86	Meatballs	43	126	Potato Wedges	63
87	Meatloaf	44	127	Ricotta Balls	64
88	Pork Chops	44	128	Roast Courgette	64
89	Pork Fillet	45	129	Roast Potatoes	65
90	Pork Pie	45	130	Spicy Corn On The Cob	65
91	Pot Roast	46	131	Stuffed Mushrooms	66
92	Roast Beef	46	132	Sweet Potato Chips	66
93	Roast Pork	47	133	Welsh Lavercakes	67
94	Rolled Brisket	47	134	Yorkshire Puddings	67
95	Salisbury Steak	48	135	Apple Crumble	68
96	Shepherd's Pie	48	136	Apple Pie	68
97	Spam Fritter Balls	49	137	Apple Turnover	69
98	Steak	49	138	Baked Oatmeal	69
99	Steak & Ale Pie	50	139	Banana Bread	70
100	Toad In The Hole	50	140	Banana Fritter	70
101	Traditional Egg & Bacon Pie	51	141	Beer Battered Mars Bar	71
102	Beer Battered Sausage	51	142	Bread Pudding	71
103	Baked Potato	52	143	Cheese Cake	72
104	Bannock	52	144	Chocolate Chip Biscuits	72
105	Bread	53	145	Doughnuts	73
106	British Stuffing	53	146	Eccles Cakes	73
107	Brussels Sprouts	54	147	Flapjacks	74
108	Bubble & Squeak	54	148	Fried Ice-cream Balls	74
109	Cabbage	55	149	Fried Pineapple	75
110	Cauliflower Cheese	55	150	Lemon Drizzle	75
111	Champ	56	151	Melting Moments	76
112	Cheesy Potatoes	56	152	Parkin	76
113	Chickpea Meatballs	57	153	Peach Cobbler	77
114	Chunky Chips	57	154	Rhubarb & Custard	77
115	Crispy Fried Tofu	58	155	Rock Cakes	78
116	Croutons	58	156	Scone Slices	78
117	Fried Grated Potato	59	157	Shortbread Biscuits	79
118	Garlic Bread	59	158	Spotted Dick	79
119	Garlic Mushrooms	60	159	Treacle Tart	80
120	Garlic Roast Potatoes	60	160	Victoria Sponge	80

Cheese Toastie

Two slices of bread, 2 slices of cheese, or 120 g (4 oz) grated cheddar cheese, 15 g (1 tbsp) salted butter, and ground black pepper to taste.

Spread butter on one side of each slice of bread. Next, place the cheese on each unbuttered side and fold them together to make a sandwich. Next, place the sandwich in the air fryer and cook for 4 minutes at 200C (400F) or until the toast is brown and the cheese has melted.

Crumpets

400 ml (1 1/2 cups/14 oz) milk, 9 g (1 tbsp) dried yeast, 4 g (1 tsp) caster sugar, 300 g (2 1/2 cups/10 oz) sieved plain flour, 3 g (1/2 tsp) bicarbonate of soda, 5 g (1 tsp) fine sea salt, and vegetable oil spray.

Warm the milk. Dissolve the yeast and the sugar in the warm milk and 100 ml (3 1/2 oz) of slightly warm water. Leave the mixture warm for about 10 minutes or until frothy. Mix the flour, salt, and bicarbonate of soda in a bowl. Make a well in the mixture and add the yeast mix. Whisk from the centre until the mixture is as thick as double cream, and if needed, add a little water. Cover with a damp cloth and leave for 45 minutes or until it starts to get little bubbles forming on the surface. Preheat the air fryer to 200C (400F). Grease four 10 cm (4 inch) egg rings with vegetable oil. Spray a little oil into a non-porous air fryer basket and place the rings into it—spoon 120 g (4 tbsp/4 oz) of the mixture into each ring. Cook for about 5 minutes or until little bubbles appear on the surface. Once the bubbles have burst, use tongs to lift off the rings, flip the crumpets over and cook for 1 minute. Continue with another batch.

Devilled Eggs

Six large eggs, 30 ml (2 tbsp/1 oz) mayonnaise, 5 ml (1 tsp) Dijon mustard, 1.5 g (1/4 tsp) salt, .5 g (1/4 tsp) pepper, and paprika for garnish.

Place the eggs in their shells in the air fryer basket and set the temperature to 190C (375F). Cook for 12 minutes. Remove the eggs from the air fryer and place them in a bowl of ice water for 5 minutes (like all recipes, times may vary depending on the air fryer). Peel the eggs and slice them in half lengthwise. Remove the yolks and place them in a separate bowl. Mash the yolks with a fork and add the mayonnaise, mustard, salt, and pepper. Mix well. Pipe the yolk mixture back into the egg white halves using a piping or a plastic bag with the corner snipped off. Sprinkle the eggs with paprika. Return to the air fryer for 3 minutes at 190C (375F).

Eggy Bread

Two slices of bread, 2 eggs, 30 ml (2 tbsp/1 oz) milk, salt and pepper to taste, and 15 ml (1 tbsp/1/2 oz) butter or olive oil.

Crack the eggs into a shallow dish and beat them with a fork. Add the milk, salt, and pepper to the eggs and beat until well combined. Melt the butter or heat the oil in a frying pan over medium heat. Dip each slice of bread into the egg mixture, ensuring both sides are coated. Place the coated slices of bread in the air fryer basket and set the temperature to 200C (400F). Cook for 8-10 minutes or until the bread is golden brown and crispy.

Full English Breakfast

Two chunky pork or pork and beef sausages (aka bangers), 2 rashers of bacon, 2 eggs, 2 slices of black pudding, 1 tomato, baked beans, a handful of sliced mushrooms and 2 slices of bread.

Place the sausages, bacon, tomato cut in half, mushrooms, and black pudding in the air fryer. Give them a little spray with cooking oil and cook for 10 minutes at 180C (350F). Next, lift out the food and soak up the oils and grease in the air fryer from the meats with the two slices of bread. Place the food back into the air fryer. Add a small ramekin-sized bowl of baked beans. Place the bread on a firm surface and firmly press an indent with the bottom of a glass. Place a rack above the meats, tomato, and mushrooms, and place the bread on the rack. Now, gently crack an egg into a bowl and pour it onto one of the slices of bread in the indentation so that it doesn't flow over the edges. Do the same with the other slice of bread and egg. Cook the lot for 5 more minutes or until the egg is done to your liking and the bread is toast.

Hard Boiled Eggs

Four to six large eggs.

Preheat the air fryer to 140C (270F). If there are no such low settings, go for 150C (300F). Add the eggs to the air fryer basket and leave some space between each egg. For soft-boiled eggs, cook for 9-11 minutes, not-so-runny eggs; 12-13, hard-boiled eggs; 13-15 minutes. If your air fryer can only be set to 150C (300F), subtract about 1 or 2 minutes. You might need some practice figuring out how long to cook the eggs in your air fryer. While the eggs are cooking, it is time to prepare an ice bath. Half-fill a bowl with ice. Add cold water until the bowl has enough room for eggs without overflowing. Once cooked, place the eggs in the ice bath until they are cool but not ice cold. Crack the eggshells and roll them along a hard surface to shatter the shell. Peel and enjoy or refrigerate.

No Mess Egg On Toast

One slice of your favourite thick bread, 1 egg, salt and pepper to taste, and cooking oil spray.

Preheat your air fryer to 180C (350F). Spray inside the air fryer basket with cooking oil, or spray a trivet rack with the oil. Place the bread on a hard surface and press a shape firmly and deeply into it. It could be the bottom of a cup, or press your finger or thumb to make the shape deep and large enough to contain the egg. Cracking the egg onto the bread might be messy, so break the egg into a bowl and season with salt and pepper. Place the bread into the air fryer and pour the egg gently into the indentation on the bread. Cook in the air fryer for 7-8 minutes or until the eggs are cooked to your desired level and the bread is toast.

Poached Eggs

Three large eggs, 30 ml (2 tbsp/1 oz) water, 5 ml (1 tsp) white vinegar, salt and pepper to taste.

Preheat your air fryer to 180C (350F). Crack the eggs into separate small bowls. Pour the water, vinegar, and a pinch of salt into the air fryer basket. Carefully add the egg bowls one at a time into the basket, ensuring they do not touch each other. Cook for 8 minutes. Remove the poached eggs from the bowls and season with salt and pepper to taste.

Scrapple

225 g (8 oz) pork sausage, 60 g (1/2 cup/2 oz) white cornmeal, 30 g (1/4 cup/1 oz) whole wheat flour, 2 g (1 tsp) garlic powder, 2 g (1 tsp) onion powder, 1 g (1/2 tsp) black pepper, 3 g (1/2 tsp) salt, .5 g (1/4 tsp) baking powder, 30 ml (2 tbsp/1 oz) water, and 60 ml (1/4 cup/2 oz) vegetable oil.

Combine the sausage, cornmeal, flour, garlic powder, onion powder, black pepper, salt, and baking powder in a large bowl. Stir in the water and mix until everything is evenly combined. Shape the mixture into round patties, about 7.5 - 10 cm (3 - 4 inch) diameter rounds. Heat the vegetable oil in an air fryer at 180C (350F) for 5 minutes. Place the patties in the air fryer basket and cook for 10 minutes, flipping halfway through.

Welsh Rarebit

Two slices of bread, 200g (7 oz) grated cheddar cheese, 30 g (2 tbsp/3 oz) butter, 15 g (2 tbsp/1/2 oz) plain flour, 150 ml (5 oz) milk, 15 ml (1 tbsp/1/2 oz) Worcestershire sauce, 2 g (1 tsp) dry mustard powder, and salt and pepper to taste.

Preheat the air fryer to 200C (390F). In a saucepan, melt the butter over medium heat. Stir in the flour to form a paste, and cook for 1 minute. Gradually add the milk, constantly whisking, until the mixture is smooth and thick. Remove the saucepan from the heat and stir in the grated cheddar cheese until it melts. Next, stir in the Worcestershire sauce, mustard powder, salt, and pepper. Toast the bread in the air fryer for 2-3 minutes or until golden brown. Spoon the cheese sauce over the toast and return to the air fryer. Cook for 2-3 minutes or until the cheese is bubbly and golden brown.

Bacon Wrapped Pineapple

Eight rashers of bacon, 1 fresh pineapple peeled - cored and cut into lengths short enough to be wrapped in the bacon, 45 g (1/4 cup/1 1/2 oz) brown sugar, 2 g (1 tsp) chilli powder. Toothpicks.

Preheat the air fryer to 200C (400F). In a small bowl, mix brown sugar and chilli powder. Wrap each pineapple length with a slice of bacon and secure it with a toothpick. Roll each bacon-wrapped pineapple wedge in the brown sugar mixture and coat evenly. Place the wedges in the air fryer basket, making sure not to overcrowd them. Cook for 12-15 minutes, flipping halfway through until the bacon is crispy and the pineapple is tender.

Bagels

240 g (2 cups/8 1/2 oz) plain flour, 4 g (2 tsp) baking powder, 5 g (1 tsp) salt, 160 ml (2/3 cup/5 oz) warm water, 15 ml (1 tbsp/1/2 oz) olive oil, 5 ml (1 tsp) honey, and 4 g (2 tsp) active dry yeast.

Whisk together the flour, baking powder, and sea salt in a large bowl. Combine the warm water, olive oil, honey, and active dry yeast in a separate bowl. Stir until the yeast dissolves. Pour the wet ingredients into the dry ingredients and mix until a dough forms. Knead the dough for 3-5 minutes until it is elastic and no longer sticky. Divide the dough into 8 equal pieces and form each into a bagel shape. Place the bagels into the air fryer and cook at 190C (375F) for 12-15 minutes, until golden brown.

Banana Chips

Two ripe bananas, 15 ml (1 tbsp/1/2 oz) lemon juice, .5 g (1/4 tsp) ground cinnamon, and 50 g (1/4 cup/1 1/2 oz) granulated sugar.

Peel and slice the bananas about .3 cm (1/8 inch) thick. In a bowl, mix the lemon juice, cinnamon, and sugar. Add the banana slices to the bowl and toss until evenly coated. Preheat the air fryer to 150C (300F). Place the banana slices in a single layer in the air fryer basket. Cook for 10-15 minutes or until the edges are golden brown. Flip the pieces halfway through. Remove the banana chips from the air fryer and let them cool completely.

Battered Cheese Curds

For air fryer batter advice, see the Batter Splatter page.

250 ml (1 cup/9 oz) cheese curds, 30 g (1/4 cup/1 oz) plain flour, 30 g (1/4 cup/1 oz) cornflour, .5 g (1/4 tsp) garlic powder, .5 g (1/4 tsp) onion powder, 1.5 g (1/4 tsp) salt, .5 g (1/4 tsp) black pepper, 1 egg - beaten, and 25 g (1/4 cup/1 oz) Panko breadcrumbs.

Preheat the air fryer to 200C (400F). Combine flour, cornflour, garlic powder, onion powder, salt, and pepper in a large bowl. Dip cheese curds in beaten egg and then coat them in flour. Place the coated cheese curds in the air fryer basket and cook for 5-7 minutes or until golden brown and crispy. Serve warm with your favourite dipping sauce.

Battered Crab Sticks

For air fryer batter advice, see the Batter Splatter page.

340 g (12 oz) crab sticks/fish sticks, 120 g (1 cup/4 oz) plain flour, 3 g (1/2 tsp) salt, 2 g (1 tsp) paprika, 1 g (1/2 tsp) garlic powder, 1 g (1/2 tsp) onion powder, .5 g (1/4 tsp) black pepper, 250 g (1 cup/9 oz) beer, and a little olive oil for brushing.

Preheat the air fryer to 200C (400F). Mix the flour, salt, paprika, garlic powder, onion powder, and black pepper in a large bowl. Slowly pour in the beer and mix until the batter is smooth. Dip the crab sticks into the batter, coating evenly. Brush the air fryer basket with oil. Place the battered crab sticks in the basket, making sure not to overcrowd them. Cook for 5 minutes before turning over and cooking for 4 minutes or until golden brown and crispy.

Blooming Onion

One large onion, 120 g (1 cup/4 oz) plain flour, 2 g (1 tsp), 2 g (1 tsp) paprika, 2 g (1 tsp) onion powder, 3 g (1/2 tsp), 2 g (1 tsp) ground black pepper, 125 ml (1/2 cup/4 1/2) beer, 30 g (1/4 cup/1 oz) panko breadcrumbs or crustless breadcrumbs if unable to get panko.

Preheat the air fryer to 180C (350F). Peel the onion and cut off the top. Cut the onion into segments without going through so the onion remains intact. Carefully separate the segments so you get a blooming onion shape. Mix the flour, garlic powder, paprika, onion powder, salt, and pepper in a medium bowl. In a separate bowl, whisk together the beer and panko breadcrumbs. Dip each onion segment into the flour and beer mixture and then back into the flour mixture. Make sure the onion is coated. Place the onion in the air fryer basket. Cook for 10 minutes, flipping the onion halfway through.

Breaded Cheese Sticks

60 g (1/4 cup/2 oz) plain flour, 2 beaten eggs, 90 g (2/3 cup/3 oz) breadcrumbs, 1 g (1/2 tsp) garlic powder, 1 g (1/2 tsp) Italian seasoning, 1.5 g (1/4 tsp) salt, .5 g (1/4 tsp) ground black pepper, 60 g (1/2 cup/2 oz) grated Parmesan, 6 mozzarella or cheddar string cheese sticks.

Preheat the air fryer to 200C (400F). Put the flour into a shallow bowl. Place the eggs into a separate shallow bowl. Combine the breadcrumbs, garlic powder, Italian seasoning, salt, pepper, and Parmesan cheese in a third shallow bowl. Dip each cheese stick into the flour, eggs, and breadcrumb mixture, ensuring the cheese is coated. Place the coated mozzarella sticks in the air fryer basket. Cook for 4 minutes, then flip them over. Cook until golden brown and the cheese is melted. Serve with your favourite dip.

Carrot Chips

Four medium carrots - peeled and sliced into thin rounds with a knife or crinkle cutter, 15 ml (1 tbsp) olive oil, and salt and pepper to taste.

Preheat your air fryer to 200C (400F). Toss the sliced carrots with olive oil, salt, and pepper in a large bowl. Spread the carrots in a single layer in the basket of your air fryer. Cook the carrots for 10-12 minutes or until they are crispy and golden brown, flipping them halfway through cooking. Remove the carrot chips from the air fryer and serve.

Cauliflower Bites

For air fryer batter advice, see the Batter Splatter page.

One head of cauliflower, 60 g (1/2 cup/2 oz) plain flour, 125 ml (1/2 cup/4 1/2 oz) water, 60 ml (1/4 cup/2 oz) spicy sauce, 30 ml (2 tbsp/1 oz) olive oil, 1 g (1/2 tsp) garlic powder, 2 g (1 tsp) paprika, 1 g (1/2 tsp) onion powder, 1 g (1/2 tsp) black pepper, 1 g (1/2 tsp) cayenne pepper.

Preheat the air fryer to 200C (400F). Cut the cauliflower into florets, discarding the stem and leaves. Mix the flour and water in a medium bowl to make a batter. Dip each cauliflower floret in the batter and shake off the excess. Place the florets in the air fryer and cook for 15 minutes or until golden brown and crispy. Mix the hot sauce, olive oil, garlic powder, paprika, onion powder, black pepper, and cayenne in a small bowl. Remove the cooked cauliflower from the air fryer and place it in the bowl with the hot sauce mixture. Toss to combine. Place the coated cauliflower back in the air fryer and cook for 5 minutes. Serve warm with a dip of your choice.

Cheese Stuffed Burger

500 g (1 lb 1 oz) minced beef, 140 g (1 cup/5 oz) grated cheddar cheese, 60 g (1/4 cup/2 oz) diced onion, 2 g (1 tsp) finely grated garlic, 3 g (1/2 tsp) salt, .5 g (1/4 tsp) black pepper, 1 beaten egg.

Combine minced beef, diced onion, garlic, salt, pepper, and beaten egg in a mixing bowl. Mix well. Divide the mixture into 8 equal portions. Take one part of the mixture and flatten it into a patty. Place 30 g (2 tbsp/1 oz) of shredded cheese in the centre of the patty. Take another portion of the mixture and flatten it into a patty. Place it on the cheese-filled patty and press the edges to seal the cheese inside. Repeat the process with the remaining portions of the mixture. Refrigerate for 1 hour. Preheat your air fryer to 200C (400F). Place the stuffed burgers in the air fryer basket and cook for 12-15 minutes or until the internal temperature reaches 70C (160F).

Chicken Wings

1 kg (2 lb 2 oz) chicken wings, 30 ml (2 tbsp/1 oz) olive oil, 4 g (2 tsp) garlic powder, 4 g (2 tsp) onion powder, 4 g (2 tsp) smoked paprika, 6 g (1 tsp) sea salt, and 1 g (1/2 tsp) black pepper.

Preheat the air fryer to 190C (375F). Combine chicken wings, olive oil, garlic powder, onion powder, smoked paprika, sea salt, and black pepper in a large bowl. Toss to combine. Place chicken wings in the air fryer basket in a single layer. Cook for 20 minutes, flipping halfway through. Serve hot with your favourite dipping sauce.

Cornish Pasty

Enough ready-made shortcrust pastry for four squares 20x20 cm (8x8 inch). 200 g (1 cup/7 oz) diced potatoes, 100 g (1/2 cup/3 1/2 oz) diced carrots, 70 g (1/2 cup/2 oz) diced onion, 100 g (1/2 cup/3 1/2 oz) diced rutabaga or turnip or swede. 100 g (1/2 cup/3 1/2 oz) minced or cubed beef or lamb, 1 egg - beaten, and salt and pepper to taste.

Preheat the air fryer to 200C (390F). Mix the potatoes, carrots, onion, rutabaga, beef or lamb, egg, salt, and pepper in a large bowl. Place about 70 g (1/4 cup/3 oz) of the mixture onto one-half of each pastry square. Fold the pastry over the filling and press the edges around the filling into a crescent shape to seal, then trim off the excess. Roll up the edges to seal. Brush the top of each pasty with a beaten egg and knife a small hole in it. Place the pasties in the air fryer basket and cook for 20-30 minutes until the pastry is golden brown and cooked.

Crispy Chickpeas

400 g (14 oz) canned chickpeas drained and rinsed, 15 ml (1 tbsp/1/2 oz) olive oil, 2 g (1 tsp) ground cumin, 1 g (1/2 tsp), and salt and pepper to taste.

Preheat your air fryer to 200C (400F). Mix the olive oil, cumin, garlic powder, salt, and pepper in a bowl. Add the chickpeas and toss to coat in the mix. Place the chickpeas in the air fryer basket and cook for 20-25 minutes, shaking the basket every 6-10 minutes until crispy.

Crispy Pizza

3 ml (1/2 tsp) olive oil, 1 pre-made pizza crust, 180 ml (3/4 cup/6 oz) pizza sauce, 115 g (1 cup/6 1/2 oz) shredded mozzarella, 60 g (1/2 cup/2 oz) grated cheddar cheese, and desired toppings.

A British favourite since 1965 or earlier. Preheat your air fryer to 200C (400F). Grease the air fryer basket with olive oil. Place the pizza crust in the basket and spread the pizza sauce over it. Sprinkle the grated mozzarella and cheddar cheese over the sauce. Add your desired pizza toppings. Place the basket in the air fryer and cook at 200C (400F) for 8-10 minutes or until the cheese is melted and bubbly. Carefully remove the basket from the air fryer.

Flowered Cauliflower

For air fryer batter advice, see the Batter Splatter page.

One head of cauliflower cut into florets, 60 g (1/2 cup/2 oz) plain flour, 50 g (1/2 cup/2 oz) grated Parmesan cheese, 30 g (1/4 cup/1 oz) finely grated onion, 1 large egg, 1 g (1/2 tsp) garlic powder, salt and pepper to taste, and cooking spray.

Preheat the air fryer to 200C (400F). In a food processor, pulse cauliflower florets until they are fine and resemble rice. Mix cauliflower rice, flour, Parmesan cheese, onion, egg, garlic powder, salt, and pepper in a large bowl. Using your hands, form the mixture into tiny cylindrical shapes or rounds. Spray them with cooking spray and place them in the air fryer basket. Cook for 12-15 minutes, flipping halfway through, until golden brown and crispy.

Fried Pickles

For air fryer batter advice, see the Batter Splatter page.

Two big dill pickles sliced into .7 cm (1/4 inch) slices (or crinkle cut), 35 g (1/4 cup/1 1/2 oz) plain flour, 1 g (1/2 tsp) garlic powder, 1 g (1/2 tsp) onion powder, 1 g (1/2 tsp) paprika, 1 g (1/2 tsp) black pepper, 60 ml (1/4 cup/2 oz) buttermilk, 25 g (1/4 cup/1 oz) panko breadcrumbs, 12 g (2 tbsp) grated Parmesan, 1 g (1/2 tsp) Italian seasoning, 1 g (1/2 tsp) cayenne.

Preheat the air fryer to 190C (375F). Mix the flour, garlic powder, onion powder, paprika, and black pepper in a shallow dish. Mix the buttermilk, panko breadcrumbs, Parmesan, Italian seasoning, and cayenne in a separate shallow dish. Dip the pickles slices in the flour mixture and shake off any excess. Dip the pickles in the buttermilk mixture and coat both sides. Place the pickles in the air fryer basket in a single layer. Cook for 10 minutes, flipping halfway.

Grilled Cheese In Milk

500 g (1 lb 1 oz) mature cheddar - cut into 2.5 cm (1 inch) cubes, milk, and a pinch of pepper.

Place the cubed cheese on a baking tray or heatproof dish to fit the air fryer comfortably, ensuring the cubes are at least 2.5 cm (1 inch) between them but no more than 5 cm (2 inch) apart. Pour the milk into the tray but not over the cheese. Only pour enough milk to a depth of 1.3 cm (1/2 inch). Once the milk is poured, lift each cube of cheese up and down, allowing the milk to get under each cube so the cheese will not stick to the tray. Sprinkle a little black pepper over the milk and cheese, and cook in the air fryer for 5 minutes at 200C (400F) or until the cheese has melted into the milk and gone either light or dark brown, not burnt on the surface. Remove and serve warm with chunky dipping bread and a fork to extract the cheese.

Macaroni Cheese

225 g (8 oz) elbow macaroni, 500 ml (2 cups/17 oz) milk, 60 g (4 tbsp/2 oz) butter, 60 g (4 tbsp/2 oz) flour, 6 g (1 tsp) salt, and 280 g (2 cups/10 oz) grated cheddar cheese.

Cook macaroni according to package instructions until al dente. In a separate saucepan, melt butter over medium heat. Stir in flour and salt to create a thick sauce. Slowly pour in milk while whisking the mixture to prevent clumping. Cook the sauce for 2-3 minutes or until it thickens. Stir in shredded cheese until melted. Add cooked macaroni to the cheese sauce and mix well. Transfer the macaroni and cheese to an air fryer-safe dish. Cook in the air fryer at 190C (375F) for 10-15 minutes or until the top is crispy.

Meatball Roll

One package of frozen meatballs, or make your own using our recipe (page 35), 1 jar of your favourite marinara sauce, 60 g (1/2 cup/2 oz) grated mozzarella cheese, 4 sub rolls, and 30 ml (2 tbsp) olive oil.

Preheat your air fryer to 200C (400F). Place the frozen meatballs in the air fryer basket. Cook for 8-10 minutes or until the meatballs are cooked. Meanwhile, heat the marinara sauce in a small saucepan. When the meatballs are ready, transfer them to the saucepan and mix them with the marinara sauce. Cut the rolls in half but only some way through, then spread some meatball mixtures on each. Sprinkle the mozzarella cheese over the subs, then drizzle with the olive oil. Place the rolls in the air fryer basket and cook at 200C (400F) for 8-10 minutes, until the cheese is melted and the rolls golden brown.

Nut Loaf

300 g (2 cups/11 oz) walnuts - crushed, 150 g (1 cup/5 oz) pecans - crushed, 150 g (1 cup/5 oz) almonds - crushed, 150 g (1 cup/5 oz) unsweetened shredded coconut, 50 g (1/2 cup/2 oz) oat flour, 2 g (1 tsp) ground cinnamon, 2 g (1 tsp) ground nutmeg, 1 g (1/2 tsp) ground ginger, 1 g (1/4 tsp) ground cloves, 3 g (1/2 tsp) salt, 125 ml (1/2 cup/4 oz) maple syrup, 30 ml (2 tbsp/1 oz) melted coconut oil and 10 ml (2 tsp) vanilla extract.

Preheat the air fryer to 190C (375F). Combine the walnuts, pecans, almonds, shredded coconut, oat flour, cinnamon, nutmeg, ginger, cloves, and salt in a medium bowl. Mix until combined. Whisk together the maple syrup, coconut oil, and vanilla extract in a small bowl. Pour the wet ingredients into the dry ingredients and mix until evenly incorporated. Grease a 20x10 cm (8x4 inch) loaf pan with coconut oil. Transfer the nut loaf batter to the loaf pan and spread it out evenly. Place the loaf pan in the preheated air fryer and cook for 25 minutes.

Onion Rings

For air fryer batter advice, see the Batter Splatter page.

One large onion - sliced into thick rings, 60 g (1/2 cup/2 oz) plain flour, 60 g (1/2 cup/2 oz) cornflour, 6 g (1 tsp) salt, 2 g (1 tsp) garlic powder, and 1 g (1/2 tsp) paprika.

Mix the flour, cornflour, salt, garlic powder and paprika in a large bowl. Dip the onion rings into the mixture. Next, place the onion rings in your air fryer on a single layer and set the temperature to 200C (400F). Cook for 10 minutes, checking every few minutes to ensure the rings don't burn. Remove from the fryer once the onion rings are crispy.

Pigs In Blankets

Twelve cocktail sausages, 6 slices of streaky bacon cut in half, and 5 ml (1 tsp) vegetable oil.

Preheat the air fryer to 200C (400F). Brush each sausage with vegetable oil and wrap half a slice of bacon. Place the wrapped sausages into the air fryer basket. Cook for 8 minutes, turning halfway through.

Popcorn Chicken

For air fryer batter advice, see the Batter Splatter page.

500 g (1 lb 1 oz) boneless skinless chicken breasts cut into bite-sized pieces, 250 ml (1 cup/9 oz) buttermilk, 120 g (1 cup/4 oz) plain flour, 4 g (2 tsp) paprika, 2 g (1 tsp) garlic powder, 3 g (1/2 tsp) salt, .5 g (1/4 tsp) black pepper, .5 g (1/4 tsp) cayenne pepper (optional), and oil spray.

Mix the buttermilk, paprika, garlic powder, salt, black pepper, and cayenne pepper (if using). Add the chicken pieces and toss to coat. Cover and marinate in the refrigerator for at least 1 hour or overnight. In a shallow dish, mix the flour, paprika, garlic powder, salt, black pepper, and cayenne pepper (if using). Remove the chicken from the marinade and let any excess drip off. Place each piece of chicken in the flour mixture, pressing the flour mixture onto the chicken to coat evenly. Spray the air fryer basket with cooking spray. Arrange the chicken in the basket, making sure not to overcrowd it. Set the air fryer to 190C (375F) and cook for 12-15 minutes until the chicken is golden brown. Shake the basket halfway through cooking.

Potato Peel Crisps

Six large potatoes, sea salt, and olive oil or cooking spray.

Wash and peel the potatoes, cutting off any eyes or blemishes. Reserve the flesh for another use. Cut the potato peelings into thin, even strips. Place the strips in a bowl and sprinkle them with sea salt. Toss to combine. Preheat the air fryer to 200C (400F). Place the potato strips in a single layer in the air fryer basket or multi-layer on a rack, making sure not to overcrowd the basket. If necessary, work in batches. Spray or brush the potato strips with olive oil or cooking spray. Fry for 10-12 minutes or until golden brown and crispy, flipping the strips halfway through cooking. Serve immediately, sprinkled with additional salt if desired.

Reuben Sandwich

Two slices of rye or brown bread of choice, 30 ml (2 tbsp/1 oz) Thousand Island dressing, 60 g (2 oz) sliced corned beef (preferably) or ham, 2 slices of Swiss cheese, and 60 g (1/4 cup/2 oz) sauerkraut.

Preheat your air fryer to 200C (400F). Spread the Thousand Island dressing on one side of each slice of bread. Place corned beef and cheese on one slice of bread, then top with sauerkraut. Place the other slice of bread on top to make a sandwich. Place the sandwich in the air fryer and cook for 6-8 minutes, until the bread is toasted and the cheese is melted.

Salt & Pepper Chips

One green pepper – diced, 1 green chilli pepper - diced, 1 onion - diced, 1 red chilli pepper– sliced, 2 g (1 tsp) garlic powder, 2 g (1 tsp) onion powder, 1 g (1/2 tsp) Chinese five-spice powder, 2 g (1 tsp) crushed Szechuan peppercorns, 15 ml (1 tbsp/1 oz) sesame oil, 15 ml (2 tbsp/1/2 oz) sweet chilli sauce, a bunch of chopped spring onions, a handful of chopped coriander.

Start with the Chunky Chips Recipe, Page 58. While the chips are cooking, take out a small baking tin or a takeaway tin and add the diced onion and red and green chilli peppers. Sprinkle the garlic powder, onion powder, Szechuan pepper, five-spice, salt, and sesame oil and give everything a good mixing, then remove the chips from the air fryer once cooked, put the ingredients in a tin, and cook them for 7-10 minutes at 200C (400F). Next, remove the ingredients from the air fryer and line the basket with tin foil. Add the chips and ingredients, drizzle the sweet chilli sauce over the top, and gently mix. Cook for 5 minutes at 200C (400F). Remove from the air fryer and add coriander, chillies, and spring onions. Serve.

Sausage Rolls

One pack of ready-made puff pastry, 226 g (8 oz) sausage meat, 2 eggs, 15 ml (1 tbsp/1/2 oz) olive oil, and salt and pepper to taste.

Preheat the air fryer to 180C (350F). Cut the puff pastry into 4-6 rectangles. Mix the sausage meat, eggs, salt, and pepper in a bowl. Divide the mixture into 4-6 portions and shape them into sausage rolls. Place the sausage rolls onto the puff pastry rectangles and roll them up. You can secure the edges with a fork so the filling is sealed. Brush the tops of the rolls with olive oil. Place the rolls into the air fryer for about 15 minutes or until golden and crispy.

Scotch Eggs

Six hard-boiled eggs - peeled, 500 g (1 lb 1 oz) sausage meat, 12 g (2 tbsp) finely chopped fresh parsley, 10 ml (2 tsp) Worcestershire sauce, 1 g (1/2 tsp) garlic powder, 1 g (1/2 tsp) onion powder, 1 g (1/2 tsp) dried thyme, 1 g (1/2 tsp) ground black pepper, 1.5 g (1/4 tsp) sea salt, 1 g (1/2 tsp) smoked paprika, 100 g (1 cup/3 1/2 oz) plain breadcrumbs and 2 beaten eggs.

Preheat your air fryer to 190C (375F). Mix the sausage meat, parsley, Worcestershire sauce, garlic powder, onion powder, thyme, pepper, salt, and smoked paprika in a bowl. Divide the mixture into 6 equal portions and shape it into patties. Place a boiled egg in the centre of each patty and wrap the patty around the egg. Dip each patty-wrapped egg in the beaten egg, then press into the breadcrumbs to coat. Place the eggs in the air fryer basket and cook for 12 minutes, flipping once halfway through.

Spicy Roasted Peanuts

300 g (2 cups/11 oz) unsalted peanuts, 30 ml (2 tbsp/1 oz) olive oil, 4 g (2 tsp) chilli powder, 4 g (2 tsp) garlic powder, 1 g (1/2 tsp) ground cumin, and 3 g (1/2 tsp) sea salt.

Preheat the air fryer to 180C (350F). Combine peanuts, olive oil, chilli powder, garlic powder, cumin, and sea salt in a medium bowl. Stir until peanuts are evenly coated. Place peanuts in an air fryer basket and spread them into an even layer. Cook for 12-15 minutes, shaking the basket halfway through until the peanuts are golden brown and crispy.

Sweet Potato Crisps

Two medium sweet potatoes - peeled or skins on and cut into .5 cm (1/5 inch) thick slices, 30 ml (2 tbsp/1 oz) olive oil, 1 g (1/2 tsp) garlic powder, 1 g (1/2 tsp) paprika, 1 g (1/2 tsp) onion powder, 3 g (1/2 tsp) salt.

Preheat the air fryer to 190C (375F). Place sweet potatoes in a large bowl and drizzle with olive oil. Add garlic powder, paprika, onion powder and salt, and toss to coat. Place sweet potatoes in a single layer in the air fryer basket. Cook for 15 minutes, flipping halfway through.

Thin Cut Fries

Four Russet potatoes - peeled and patted dry, 3 g (1/2 tsp) salt, and 12 ml (1 tbsp) olive oil.

Start by cutting the potatoes into slices and placing them in a bowl. Mix the olive oil, salt, and sliced potatoes well. Place the potatoes into the air fryer basket and set the temperature to 200C (400F). Cook for about 15 minutes or until golden brown.

Thin Kale Chips

One bunch of kale, 15 ml (1 tbsp/1/2 oz) olive oil, and salt and pepper to taste.

Preheat your air fryer to 190C (375F). Remove the kale leaves from the thick stems and tear them into bite-sized pieces. Toss the kale in a bowl with olive oil, salt, and pepper. Place the kale in a single layer in the air fryer basket. Cook for 8-10 minutes until the kale is crispy.

Chicken Tikka Masala

This dish is a top ten British favourite. 500 g (1 lb 1 oz) boneless skinless chicken breasts cut into bite-sized pieces, 250 ml (1 cup/9 oz) plain yoghurt, 30 ml (2 tbsp/1 oz) lemon juice, 10 g (2 tbsp) garam masala, 4 g (2 tsp) ground cumin, 2 g (1 tsp) ground turmeric, 2 g (1 tsp) ground coriander, 2 g (1 tsp) cayenne pepper, 6 g (1 tsp) salt, 60 ml (1/4 cup/2 oz) vegetable oil, 1 onion - finely chopped, 4 cloves (12 g) finely grated garlic, 12 g (2 tbsp) grated ginger, 250 ml (1 cup/9 oz) tomato puree, 250 ml (1 cup/9 oz) heavy cream, and a little fresh coriander chopped for garnish.

In a large bowl, combine the yoghurt, lemon juice, garam masala, cumin, turmeric, coriander, cayenne pepper (if using), and salt. Add the chicken and toss to coat. Cover and refrigerate for at least 2 hours or overnight. Heat the oil in a large saucepan over medium heat. Add the onion and cook until softened - about 5 minutes. Add the garlic and ginger and cook for another minute. Stir in the tomato puree and bring to a simmer. Add the mixture from the saucepan to an air fryer-safe baking dish and cook for 5 minutes at 200C (400F). Add the marinated chicken and cook for 10 more minutes until the chicken is cooked. Stir in the cream and cook for 5 minutes at 140C (275F). Garnish with fresh coriander and serve over rice.

White Rice

225 g (1 cup/8 oz) long grain rice - basmati or jasmine, 300 g (1 1/4 cup/10 oz) boiling water, and optional salt.

Rinse the rice in a fine mesh strainer until the water runs clear. Add the rinsed rice to a baking tin and the boiled water from a saucepan with a pinch of salt. Cover the baking tin with tinfoil and place the tin in the air fryer basket. Set the air fryer to 175 (350F) and cook for 18-20 minutes until the water has been absorbed and the rice is cooked through. Fluff the rice with a fork and serve.

Cock-A-Leekie Soup

One large chicken breast, 2 large leeks - sliced, 2 stalks of celery - sliced, half a cup of dried prunes (optional). 240 ml (1 cup/8 1/2 oz) chicken stock, 240 ml (1 cup/8 1/2 oz) water, 2 g (1 tsp) dried thyme, 1 bay leaf, and salt and pepper to taste.

Cut the chicken breast into bite-sized pieces and season with salt and pepper. In a large bowl, combine the chicken, leeks, celery, prunes, chicken stock, water, thyme, bay leaf, and salt and pepper to taste. Place the mixture into the air fryer in a heatproof dish, ensuring not to overcrowd it. Cook at 200C (400F) for 30 minutes or until the chicken is cooked and the potatoes are tender. Remove the bay leaf and serve the soup hot.

Cullen Skink

60 g (2 tbsp/2 oz) butter, 1 medium onion - diced, 1 large potato - peeled and diced, 2 cloves (6 g) garlic - finely grated, 125 ml (1/2 cup/4 1/2 oz) water, 125 ml (1/2 cup/4 1/2 oz) heavy cream, 3 g (1/2 tsp) salt, .5 g (1/4 tsp) black pepper, 85 g (3 oz) smoked haddock - cut into cubes, 45 g (1/4 cup/2 oz) frozen sweet corn, and 8 g (2 tbsp) chopped fresh parsley.

Preheat the air fryer to 190C (375F). Place butter in a baking or casserole dish in the air fryer and melt for 2-3 minutes. Add onion, potato, and garlic and cook for 7-8 minutes, stirring occasionally. Add the water, cream, salt, and pepper and stir. Add smoked haddock, frozen corn, and parsley and cook for 5 minutes.

Irish Stew

700 g (1 lb 8 oz) mutton or lamb, cut into 2.5 cm (1-inch) cubes, 2 medium onions - chopped, 3 medium carrots - peeled and sliced, 3 medium potatoes - peeled and chopped, 2 cloves (6 g) garlic - finely grated, 500 ml (2 cups/18 oz) beef stock, 30 ml (2 tbsp/1 oz) tomato paste, 15 g (2 tbsp/1 oz) plain flour, 30 ml (2 tbsp/1 oz) olive oil, 2 g (1 tsp) dried thyme, 2 g (1 tsp) dried rosemary, 6 g (1 tsp) salt, and 1 g (1/2 tsp) black pepper.

Preheat your air fryer to 200C (400F). Mix the flour, salt, pepper, thyme, and rosemary in a bowl. Toss the meat in the flour mixture to coat. Combine the meat, onions, carrots, potatoes, garlic, tomato paste, and olive oil in a large heatproof bowl. Place the bowl into the air fryer and cook for 20 minutes. Stir in the stock and cook for 20 minutes or until the meat is cooked through and the vegetables are tender.

Lancashire Hot Pot

500 g (1 lb 1 oz) diced lamb shoulder or leg meat, 2 large onions - sliced, 2 cloves (6 g) finely grated garlic, 60 ml (1/4 cup/2 oz) tomato paste, 500 ml (2 cups/17 1/2 oz) lamb or beef stock, 2 g (1 tsp) dried thyme, 2 g (1 tsp) dried rosemary, 2 large potatoes - sliced, and salt and pepper, to taste.

Preheat the air fryer to 200C (400F). Mix the diced lamb, onions, garlic, tomato paste, stock, thyme, rosemary, salt, and pepper in a large bowl. Layer the sliced potatoes on the bottom of a cast iron pan or oven-proof dish that fits in your air fryer. Pour the lamb mixture over the potatoes. Place the pan or dish in the air fryer for 30-40 minutes until the lamb is cooked and the potatoes are crisp around the edges and tender in the centre.

Scouse

30 ml (2 tbsp/1 oz) vegetable oil, 2 large onions - chopped, 2 large carrots - chopped, 2 celery stalks, 2 cloves (6 g) garlic - finely grated, 30 ml (2 tbsp/1 oz) tomato paste, 15 ml (1 tbsp/1/2 oz) Worcestershire sauce, 500 ml (2 cups/18 oz) beef or lamb stock, 12 g (2 tbsp) chopped fresh parsley, 2 bay leaves, 500 g (1 lb 1 oz) lean beef or lamb or both - cubed or any minor cuts you have, 500 g (1 lb 1 oz) potatoes - peeled and chopped, 6 g (1 tsp), and 1 g (1/2 tsp) ground black pepper.

Preheat your air fryer to 180C (350F). Heat the oil in a large frying pan over medium heat. Add the onions, carrots, celery, and garlic and cook, occasionally stirring, until softened, about 5 minutes. Add the tomato paste and Worcestershire sauce and cook for 1 minute more. Add the stock, parsley, and bay leaves and boil. Reduce the heat to low and simmer for 5 minutes. Add the meat, potatoes, salt, and pepper. Simmer for 10 minutes, stirring occasionally. Transfer the scouse to the air fryer in a suitable dish and cook for 15 minutes, stirring halfway.

Welsh Cawl

1 kg (2 lb 2 oz) lamb or beef - diced, 4 medium potatoes - peeled and diced, 4 medium carrots - peeled and diced, 2 medium leeks - sliced, 1 l (4 cups/35 oz) chicken or beef stock, 15 ml (1 tbsp/1/2 oz) olive oil, and salt and pepper to taste.

Toss the diced meat with salt, pepper, and olive oil in a large bowl. Place the seasoned meat in the air fryer in a large heatproof dish and cook at 200C (400F) for 8-10 minutes or until browned. Remove the browned meat from the dish and set it aside. Add the diced potatoes, carrots, and leeks to the same word. Cook at 200C (400F) for 10-12 minutes or until slightly softened. Return the browned meat to the dish and add the stock. Stir to combine. Cook at 200C (400F) for 20-25 minutes until the vegetables are tender and the stock is hot.

Baked Cod

500 g (1 lb 1 oz) cod fillets, 15 ml (1 tbsp/1/2 oz) olive oil, salt and pepper to taste, and 1 sliced lemon.

Preheat the air fryer to 200C (400F). Rub the cod with olive oil and season with salt and pepper. Place the cod in the air fryer basket, ensuring there is no overcrowded. If desired, place lemon slices on top of the fish. Cook the cod for 8-10 minutes or until the fish flakes.

Baked Monkfish

500 g (1 lb 1 oz) monkfish fillets, 1 lemon - juiced, 30 ml (2 tbsp/1 oz) olive oil, 2 cloves (6 g) finely grated, 2 g (1 tsp) dried thyme, 2 g (1 tsp) dried basil, 1 g (1/2 tsp) dried oregano, and salt and black pepper to taste.

Preheat the air fryer to 200C (400F). Mix the lemon juice, olive oil, garlic, thyme, basil, oregano, salt, and pepper in a small bowl. Place the monkfish fillets in a shallow dish and pour the marinade over them, ensuring they are well coated. Allow the monkfish to marinate for 10 minutes. Place the monkfish fillets in the air fryer in a heatproof dish, leaving some space between each piece. Bake the monkfish for 12-15 minutes or until it is opaque and flaky.

Baked Salmon

500 g (1 lb 1 oz) fresh salmon, 30 ml (2 tbsp) olive oil, 10 ml (2 tsp) honey, 4 g (1 tsp) garlic - finely grated, and salt and pepper to taste.

Preheat the air fryer to 200C (400F). Place the salmon in the air fryer basket. Mix olive oil, honey, garlic, salt, and pepper in a small bowl. Brush the salmon with the mixture. Cook for 8-10 minutes until the salmon is cooked and lightly browned.

Baked Squid

500 g (1 lb 1 oz) squid tubes - cleaned and sliced into rings, 30 ml (2 tbsp/1 oz) olive oil, 5 g (1 tsp) sea salt, 2 g (1 tsp) black pepper, 2 g (1 tsp) dried oregano, 2 g (1 tsp) dried thyme, and 2 g (1 tsp) garlic powder.

Mix the olive oil, salt, pepper, oregano, thyme, and garlic powder in a bowl. Add the sliced squid to the bowl and toss to coat evenly with the spices and oil. Place the squid in a single layer in the air fryer basket, ensuring they don't overlap. Set the temperature to 200C (400F) and cook for 8-10 minutes or until the squid is tender.

Breaded Scampi

500 g (1 lb 1 oz) large raw langoustines - peeled and deveined (as the word scampi referred to peeled prawn tails, you might also use prawns for this if langoustines are unavailable), salt and pepper to taste, 1 egg - beaten, 150 g (1 cup/5 oz) fine white breadcrumbs, 120 g (1 cup/4 oz) plain flour, and 30 ml (2 tbsp/1 oz) olive oil.

Season the peeled tails with salt and pepper. Place the beaten egg in a shallow dish. In a separate shallow dish, mix the breadcrumbs and flour. Dip each tail into the egg mixture, then coat it in the breadcrumb mixture, ensuring it's evenly coated. Place the breaded tails in the air fryer basket in a single layer. Drizzle the olive oil over the tails. Air fry at 200C (400F) for 10 minutes or until the breading is golden brown and the tails are cooked.

Coconut Prawns

For air fryer batter advice, see the Batter Splatter page.

500 g (1 lb 1 oz) of large prawns - peeled to the tail fins and deveined, 85 g (3/4 cup/3 oz) shredded coconut, 30 ml (2 tbsp/1 oz) olive oil, 2 g (1 tsp) garlic powder, 2 g (1 tsp) onion powder, 3 g (1/2 tsp) sea salt, and .5 g (1/4 tsp) of black pepper.

Preheat your air fryer to 190C (375F). In a medium bowl, combine the shredded coconut, olive oil, garlic powder, onion powder, sea salt and black pepper. Add the prawns to the bowl and mix until they are all evenly coated. Place the prawns in the air fryer basket in a single layer. Cook for 8-10 minutes or until golden brown on the outside and cooked through.

Fish Cakes

500 g (1 lb 1 oz) potatoes - peeled and diced, 226 g (8 oz) white fish fillet - skinned and boned, 30 g (2 tbsp/1 oz) plain flour, 1 beaten egg, 20 g (2 tbsp/1 oz) breadcrumbs, and salt and pepper to taste.

Boil the potatoes in a large saucepan of salted water for 12-15 minutes or until tender: drain and mash. Place the fish in a food processor and pulse until finely chopped. Mix mashed potatoes, fish, flour, egg, breadcrumbs, salt, and pepper in a large bowl. Shape the mixture into 8-10 cakes. Place the fish cakes in the air fryer basket and cook at 180C (350F) for 8-10 minutes or until golden brown and crispy.

Fish Fingers

For air fryer batter advice, see the Batter Splatter page.

500 g (1 lb 1 oz) of white fish such as cod or haddock, 2 large eggs, 8 g (2 tbsp) of plain flour, 30 ml (2 tbsp/1 oz) of olive oil (plus extra for greasing), 2 g (1 tsp) paprika, .5 g (1/2 tsp) of garlic powder, 20 g (2 tbsp/1 oz) of freshly chopped parsley and salt and pepper to taste.

Preheat the air fryer to 190C (375F). Cut the fish into strips about 2.5 cm (1 inch) thick. Whisk together the eggs, flour, olive oil, paprika, garlic powder, parsley, salt and pepper in a bowl. Dip each fish strip into the egg mixture, then place them into the air fryer. Cook for 10-12 minutes, flipping halfway through. Serve with mashed potatoes or chips.

Mussels In Cream Sauce

1 kg (2 lb 2 oz) mussels - scrubbed and debearded, 2 cloves (6 g) garlic - finely grated, 1 shallot - finely grated, 250 ml (1 cup/9 oz) heavy cream, 125 ml (1/2 cup/4 1/2 oz) white wine, 30 g (2 tbsp/1 oz) butter, 12 g (2 tbsp) fresh parsley - chopped, and salt and pepper to taste.

In a large bowl, rinse the mussels thoroughly and discard any that are open and don't close when tapped. In a saucepan, heat the butter over medium heat. Add the garlic and shallot and cook until fragrant, about 2 minutes. Add the white wine and bring it to a boil. Reduce heat to low and add the cream. Stir to combine. Season the sauce with salt and pepper to taste. Arrange the mussels in a single layer in a heatproof tin or dish in the air fryer and cook at 180C (350F) for 1 minute to prepare the mussels. Pour the sauce over the mussels and cook for 8 minutes or until the mussels are fully cooked and the sauce is hot.

Chicken Cutlets

Two skinless, boneless chicken breasts, a little olive oil for brushing, and seasonings of choice.

Preheat your air fryer to 190C (375F). Then, cut each chicken breast horizontally to form two wide flat cutlets. Place the chicken cutlets into the air fryer basket and lightly brush each cutlet with olive oil. Sprinkle lightly with your favourite seasonings, such as salt, pepper, garlic powder, and Italian herbs. Cook the chicken cutlets in the air fryer for 8-10 minutes at 190C (375F), flipping them halfway through. When golden brown and cooked, remove them.

Chicken Goujons

For air fryer batter advice, see the Batter Splatter page.

500 g (1 lb 1 oz) chicken tenderloins, or you can use whole chicken breasts cut into strips, 120 g (1 cup/4 oz) plain flour, 4 g (2 tsp) paprika, 2 g (1 tsp) garlic powder, 3 g (1/2 tsp) salt, 1/2 g (1/4 tsp) black pepper, 250 ml (1 cup/8 1/2 oz) buttermilk, 1 large egg, and Oil spray.

Mix the flour, paprika, garlic powder, salt, and pepper in a shallow dish. In a separate dish, beat the egg and add the buttermilk. Dip each chicken goujon in the buttermilk mixture, then coat in the flour mixture. Place the goujons in the air fryer basket and spray them with oil. Air fry at 200C (400F) for 8-10 minutes or until golden brown and cooked through.

Chicken Honey Mustard

Four large chicken thighs, salt and pepper to taste, 30 ml (2 tbsp/1 oz) olive oil, 30 ml (2 tbsp/1 oz) honey, 30 ml (2 tbsp/1 oz) Dijon mustard, 15 ml (1 tbsp/1/2 oz) apple cider vinegar, 2 g (1 tsp) garlic powder, and 2 g (1 tsp) onion powder.

Season the chicken thighs with salt and pepper on both sides. Whisk together the olive oil, honey, Dijon mustard, apple cider vinegar, garlic powder, and onion powder in a bowl. Place the chicken thighs in the air fryer basket and brush the honey mustard mixture on both sides. Set the air fryer to 200C (400F) and cook for 15-18 minutes, flipping the chicken halfway through, until the internal temperature reaches 74C (165F).

Chicken Rissoles

500 g (1 lb 1 oz) minced chicken, 50 g (1/2 cup/2 oz) breadcrumbs, 35 g (1/4 cup/1 oz) grated Parmesan cheese, 15 g (1/4 cup/1/2 oz) chopped fresh parsley, 1 egg - beaten, 1.5 g (1/4 tsp) salt, .5 g (1/4 tsp) black pepper, and 15 ml (1 tbsp/1/2 oz) olive oil.

Mix the minced chicken, breadcrumbs, Parmesan cheese, parsley, egg, salt, and pepper in a large bowl. Shape the mixture into round patties about 5 cm (2 inch) in diameter. Place the rissoles in the air fryer basket and brush with olive oil. Set the air fryer to 200C (400F) and cook for 10-12 minutes until the rissoles are cooked through and golden brown.

Chicken Thighs

Four chicken thighs - bone-in and skin-on, salt and pepper to taste, 1 g (1/2 tsp) paprika, 1 g (1/2 tsp) garlic powder, and olive oil spray or oil to brush.

Preheat your air fryer to 200C (400F). Season the chicken thighs with salt, pepper, paprika, and garlic powder. Place the chicken thighs in the air fryer basket and lightly spray or brush them with olive oil. Cook for 20-25 minutes or until the internal temperature reaches 75C (165F). Serve hot with your favourite side dish.

Coronation Chicken

Two cooked chicken breasts - cubed, 60 ml (4 tbsp/2 oz) mayonnaise, 7 g (1 tbsp) curry powder, 30 ml (2 tbsp/1 oz) mango chutney, 25 g (2 tbsp/1 oz) raisins, 1 g (1/2 tsp) mustard powder, 30 ml (2 tbsp/1 oz) plain yoghurt, 15 ml (1 tbsp/1/2 oz) lemon juice, 1 g (1/2 tsp) paprika, and salt and pepper to taste.

Preheat the air fryer to 180C (350F). Mix mayonnaise, curry powder, mango chutney, raisins, mustard powder, yoghurt, lemon juice and paprika in a bowl. Add the cubed chicken, and stir until the chicken is evenly coated. Place the mixture in the air fryer in a heatproof dish and cook for 8 minutes, stirring halfway—season with salt and pepper to taste.

Crispy Chicken Fillets

Four skinless fresh chicken breasts, 150 g (2 cups/5 1/2 oz) crushed cornflakes, 1.5 g (1/4 tsp) salt, .5 g (1/4 tsp) pepper, 1 g (1/2 tsp) paprika, and 125 ml (1/2 cup/4 1/2 oz) mayonnaise.

Preheat the air fryer to 200C (400F). Mix the mayonnaise, paprika, salt and pepper in a bowl, dip the chicken breasts, and rub the mixture all over. Add the crushed cornflakes and dip the chicken breasts in another bowl, ensuring they are coated. Place them in the air fryer basket, cook for 20 - 25 minutes, and turn halfway through.

Fried Chicken Breasts

Four boneless skinless chicken breasts, 4 g (2 tsp) garlic powder, 4 g (2 tsp) smoked paprika, 2 g (1 tsp) onion powder, 2 g (1 tsp) black pepper, 3 g (1 tsp) salt, 30 ml (2 tbsp/1 oz) olive oil, and 60 g (1/2 cup/2 oz) plain flour.

Preheat your air fryer to 200C (400F). Mix garlic powder, smoked paprika, onion powder, black pepper, flour and salt in a shallow bowl. Dip each chicken breast in the olive oil, then coat with the seasoning mixture. Place the chicken in the air fryer basket, ensuring it is not overcrowded. Cook for 8-10 minutes, flipping the chicken halfway through. Remove when cooked through.

Hunters Chicken

Four skinless and boneless chicken breasts, 30 ml (2 tbsp/1 oz) olive oil, 4 g (2 tsp) garlic powder, 4 g (2 tsp) smoked paprika, 2 g (1 tsp) dried oregano, 2 g (1 tsp) dried thyme, 2 g (1 tsp) onion powder, 30 ml (2 tbsp/1 oz) Worcestershire sauce, 30 ml (2 tbsp/1 oz) tomato sauce, 15 ml (1 tbsp/1/2 oz) honey, and salt and pepper to taste.

Start by mixing the olive oil, garlic powder, smoked paprika, oregano, thyme, onion powder, Worcestershire sauce, tomato sauce, and honey in a bowl. Rub the mixture onto the chicken breasts and season with salt and pepper. Place the chicken breasts in the air fryer basket and cook at 190C (375F) for 12 minutes, flipping the chicken halfway through.

Parmo

500 g (1 lb 1 oz) chicken breast fillets sliced into width ways thinly (you can also use other meats which have been tenderised), 150 g (5 1/2 oz) plain flour, 2 beaten eggs, 30 ml (2 tbsp/1 oz) milk, 2 g (1 tsp) garlic powder, 2 g (1 tsp) smoked paprika, salt and pepper to taste, .5 g (1/4 tsp) cayenne pepper, .5 g (1/4 tsp) onion powder, 150 g (5 1/2 oz) breadcrumbs, and oil spray.

Mix the flour, garlic powder, smoked paprika, cayenne pepper, onion powder, salt and pepper in a shallow bowl. In another dish, mix the milk and eggs. Place the breadcrumbs in a third dish. Dip the chicken strips, the beaten egg and milk mixture, and the breadcrumbs. Preheat the air fryer to 180C (350F). Oil the base of the air fryer basket with the spray. Place the chicken in the air fryer, spray lightly with oil, and cook for 10 minutes, flipping halfway.

Bechamel Sauce

We have included bechamel sauce because it is often eaten with the above Parmo recipe, which you can see with cheese on top in the image above, and unlike most shop-bought sauces, there are no additives or other chemicals.

It is also an excellent accompaniment for other breaded or battered foods in this book. 60 g (4 tbsp/2 oz) butter, 30 g (4 tbsp/1 oz) plain flour, 500 ml (2 cups/7 1/2 oz) whole milk, 1 g (1/2 tsp) nutmeg, and salt and pepper to taste.

Melt the butter in a saucepan over medium heat. Add the flour to the melted butter and whisk together for about 2 minutes. Slowly add the milk, whisking continuously until all the milk is added and the mixture is smooth. Increase the heat to medium-high and bring the mixture to a low boil. Reduce the heat to low and simmer for about 5 minutes, stirring occasionally. Add the nutmeg, salt, and pepper and stir to combine. Taste and adjust the seasoning if desired. Serve immediately or store in the refrigerator for up to 5 days. Place the chicken Parmo into the air fryer, pour some bechamel sauce onto it, then grate cheddar cheese over the top before cooking at 180C (350F) until the cheese has melted.

Peri Peri Chicken

Four chicken portions of your choice, 30 g (2 tbsp/1 oz) Peri Peri sauce - bottled or from the recipe below. 30 (1 tbsp/1 oz) olive oil, 1 g (1 tsp) paprika, 3 g (1/2 tsp) salt, and .5 g (1/4 tsp) black pepper.

Mix the Peri Peri sauce, olive oil, paprika, salt and pepper in a large bowl. Add the chicken thighs to the bowl and toss to coat evenly. Place the chicken in the air fryer basket and cook at 200C (400F) for 18-20 minutes or until the internal temperature reaches 74C (165F). Serve the chicken with your favourite dipping sauce.

Peri Peri Sauce

We have included Peri Peri sauce because it is often eaten with the above chicken recipe. Unlike most shop-bought sauces, there are no additives or other chemicals.

10-15 bird's eye/Thai chillis - seeds removed, 2 red peppers (Bell), 4 cloves (12 g) of garlic, 30 g (2 tbsp.1 oz) lemon juice, 30 ml (2 tbsp/1 oz) white vinegar, 30 ml (2 tbsp/1 oz) olive oil, 2 g (1 tsp) paprika, 6 g (1 tsp) salt, and 1 g (1/2 tsp) black pepper.

The UK has adopted it as a favourite from Portugal and Africa. Combine the chillis, peppers, garlic, lemon juice, white vinegar, olive oil, paprika, salt and pepper in a blender or food processor. Blend until smooth. Taste and adjust the seasoning as needed. Pour the sauce into a container or bottle and store it in the refrigerator for up to two weeks. Note: This recipe can be adjusted to taste; add more or fewer chilli peppers depending on your preferred spiciness. Also, if you wish, add 2 g (1/2 tsp) of sugar to balance the acidity of the lemon juice and vinegar.

Stuffed Chicken & Bacon

Four boneless skinless chicken breasts, 4 slices of bacon, 70 g (1/2 cup/2 1/2 g) shredded cheddar cheese, 20 g (1/4 cup/1 oz) chopped parsley, 20 g (1/4 cup/1 oz) chopped chives, salt and pepper to taste, and cooking spray.

Preheat your air fryer to 200C (400FC). Cut a deep pocket into the thickest part of each chicken breast. Mix the cheese, parsley, chives, salt, and pepper in a small bowl. Stuff the mixture into the pockets of the chicken breasts. Wrap each chicken breast with a slice of bacon, securing it with toothpicks if necessary. Spray the chicken with cooking spray. Place the chicken in the air fryer basket, ensuring they are not touching. Cook for 20-25 minutes, or until the internal temperature of the chicken reaches 74C (165F), and the bacon is crispy.

Whole Roast Chicken

One whole chicken, 30 ml (2 tbsp/1 oz) olive oil, 12 g (2 tsp) salt, 2 g (1 tsp) garlic powder, 2 g (1 tsp) paprika, and 1 g (1/2 tsp) black pepper.

Preheat the air fryer to 200C (400F). Rub the chicken with olive oil and season with salt, garlic powder, paprika, and black pepper. Place the chicken in the air fryer basket and cook for 35-40 minutes or until the internal temperature reaches 74C (165F).

Turkey Crown

One turkey crown 1.5 kg (3 lb), 6 slices of bacon, salt and pepper to taste, 2 g (1 tsp) dried thyme, 2 g (1 tsp) dried rosemary, 2 g (1 tsp) garlic powder, and 30 ml (1 tbsp/1 oz) olive oil.

Remove the turkey crown from any packaging and pat dry with paper towels. Season the turkey crown with salt, pepper, thyme, rosemary, and garlic powder. Place strips of bacon over the top of the crown and secure it with toothpicks if necessary. Brush the crown with olive oil and place it in the air fryer basket, ensuring enough space around it for air to circulate. Set the air fryer to 180C (360F) and cook for 30 minutes. After 30 minutes, use a meat thermometer to check the turkey's internal temperature. It should reach a minimum temperature of 74C (165F) in the thickest part. If necessary, continue cooking, checking the temperature every 5 minutes until it reaches the required temperature. Once the turkey crown is fully cooked, remove it from the air fryer and let it rest for 10 minutes before serving.

BBQ Ribs

1.2 kg (2 lb 8 oz) pork ribs, 12 g (2 tbsp) paprika, 6 g (1 tbsp) garlic powder, 6 g (1 tbsp) onion powder, 4 g (2 tsp) dried oregano, 4 g (2 tsp) ground cumin, 2 g (1 tsp) chilli powder, 2 g (1 tsp) smoked paprika, 30 g (2 tbsp/1 oz) brown sugar, 5 g (1 tsp) coarse salt, 1 g (1/2 tsp) ground black pepper, and 60 ml (1/4 cup/2 oz) BBQ sauce for brushing on towards the end.

Preheat an air fryer to 180C (350F). Mix the paprika, garlic powder, onion powder, oregano, cumin, chilli powder, smoked paprika, brown sugar, salt, and pepper in a small bowl. Rub the spice mixture over the ribs on a baking sheet. Place the ribs in the air fryer and cook for 25 minutes. Brush the ribs with the BBQ sauce and cook for 10 minutes.

Beef Wellington

700 g (1 lb 8 oz) beef tenderloin, salt and pepper to taste, 30 ml (2 tbsp/1 oz) olive oil, 90 g (1/4 cup/3 oz) smooth liver pâté, 60 ml (1/4 cup/2 oz) Dijon mustard, 1 sheet puff pastry, 1 egg.

Preheat the air fryer to 200C (400F). Season the beef tenderloin with salt and pepper. Heat the olive oil in a frying pan over medium-high heat. Add the beef and sear for 2-3 minutes per side or until browned all over. Remove the meat from the pan and let it cool slightly. Spread the pâté over the beef tenderloin. Then spread the Dijon mustard over the pâté. Roll out the puff pastry on a lightly floured surface to a thickness of about .6 cm (1/4 inch). Place the beef tenderloin in the centre of the puff pastry. Roll the pastry around the beef, sealing the edges and trimming any excess pastry. Beat the egg and brush it all over the pastry. Place the beef wellington in the air fryer basket, and cook for 15-20 minutes, until the pastry is golden brown and the beef is cooked to your desired level of doneness. Let the beef wellington rest for 5 minutes before slicing.

Boneless Welsh Lamb

One boneless leg of lamb or shoulder of succulent Welsh lamb - trimmed and tied 1.5-2 kg (3 lb 3 oz-3 lb 4 oz), 2 cloves (6 g) garlic - finely grated, 30 ml (2 tbsp/1 oz) olive oil, 6 g (1 tbsp) dried rosemary, 2 g (1 tsp) dried thyme, salt and black pepper to taste, and 1 sliced lemon.

Preheat your air fryer to 190C (375F) for 5 minutes. Mix the garlic, olive oil, rosemary, thyme, salt, and pepper in a small bowl. Rub the mixture over the entire surface of the leg of the lamb, making sure to get it into all the crevices. Place the leg of lamb in the air fryer basket and top with the lemon slices. Cook for 20-25 minutes per 500 g (1 lb 1 oz) of lamb or until the internal temperature reaches 65C (150F) for medium-rare. Let the lamb rest before serving.

Cottage Pie

500 g (1 lb 1 oz) minced beef, 1 onion - diced, 2 cloves (6 g) garlic - finely grated, 250 ml (1 cup/8 oz) beef stock, 250 ml (1 cup/8 oz) frozen mixed vegetables, 5 ml (1 tsp) Worcestershire sauce, 2 g (1 tsp) dried thyme, 3 g (1/2 tsp) salt, 1.5 g (1/4 tsp) black pepper, 700 g (3 cups/25 oz) mashed potatoes, and 70 g (1/2 cup/2 oz) grated cheddar cheese.

In a frying pan, cook the minced beef over medium heat until browned. Drain any excess fat. Add the diced onion and garlic to the frying pan and cook for 2-3 minutes, until softened. Stir in the beef stock, frozen mixed vegetables, Worcestershire sauce, thyme, salt, and pepper. Bring the mixture to a simmer and cook for 5-7 minutes, until the vegetables are tender. Spread the beef mixture into the bottom of an air fryer-safe dish. Spread the mashed potatoes over the beef mixture. Sprinkle the cheese over the mashed potatoes. Place the dish in the air fryer and cook at 190C (375F) for 10-15 minutes or until the pie is cooked.

Crispy Pork Belly

500 g (1 lb 1 oz) pork belly, 30 ml (2 tbsp/1 oz) olive oil, 2 g (1 tsp) garlic powder, 2 g (1 tsp) smoked paprika, 6 g (1 tsp) sea salt, and 2.3 g (1 tsp) freshly cracked black pepper.

Preheat the air fryer to 190C (375F) and cut the pork belly into bite-sized cubes. Mix olive oil, garlic powder, smoked paprika, sea salt, and pepper in a medium bowl. Toss the pork belly cubes in the seasoning mix, ensuring they are each evenly coated. Place the pork belly cubes in the air fryer basket and cook for 15-20 minutes at 190C (375F), shaking the basket every 5 minutes, then once cooked, remove the pork belly cubes.

Faggots In Gravy

Onion Gravy: 15 ml (1 tbsp/1/2 oz) sunflower oil, 2 large onions - peeled then finely chopped, 8 g (1 tbsp) plain flour, 300 ml (10 oz) ale of choice, 600 ml (21 oz) hot beef stock, a dash of Worcestershire or brown sauce, and 10 g (2 tbsp) dried mixed herbs. **Faggots:** 500 g (1 lb 1 oz) lean beef mince, 100 g (3 oz) lamb's liver - finely chopped, 100 g (3 oz) streaky bacon - finely chopped, 1 small onion - peeled and grated, 2 cloves (6g) garlic - peeled and crushed, 6 g (1 tbsp) freshly chopped parsley, 4 g (2 tsp) fresh thyme leaves, 4 g (2 tsp) freshly chopped sage, 50 g (1/3 cup/1 1/2 oz) fresh white or brown breadcrumbs, and 10 ml (2 tsp) English mustard.

Onion Gravy: Heat some oil in a large saucepan. Add the onions and cook on medium heat for five minutes. Sprinkle in the flour and continue to cook, occasionally stirring, for two to three minutes. Gradually add the ale, stock, Worcestershire or brown sauce, seasonings, and dried mixed herbs, stirring as you go. Reduce the heat and let the gravy simmer for five minutes.
Faggots: Preheat the air fryer to 160C (320F). Mix the faggot ingredients in a large bowl and shape them into 12 golf-ball-sized balls. Place them in a 1.2 l (42 oz) heatproof dish and carefully pour over the gravy. Cover the dish with foil and air fry for 1 to 1 1/2 hours, checking each half hour. Fifteen minutes before the end of cooking, remove the foil and continue.

Gammon Joint

One gammon joint approx 1 kg (2 lb 2 oz), 25 g (2 tbsp/1 oz) brown sugar, 30 ml (2 tbsp/1 oz) maple syrup, 30 ml (2 tbsp/1 oz) honey, 30 ml (2 tbsp/1 oz) Dijon mustard, 30 ml (2 tbsp/1 oz) apple cider vinegar, 2 cloves (6g) garlic -finely grated, and salt and pepper to taste.

Mix the brown sugar, maple syrup, honey, mustard, vinegar, garlic, salt, and pepper in a small bowl. If the gammon has a deep fat layer, score it in a crisscross pattern. Next, place the gammon joint in the air fryer basket and brush the mixture all over the gammon.
Air fry at 200C (400F) for 20-30 minutes or until the golden brown gammon is cooked.

Lamb Chops

Eight lamb chops, 30 ml (2 tbsp/1 oz) olive oil, 2 cloves (6 g) finely grated garlic, 4 g (2 tsp) dried rosemary, 2 g (1 tsp) dried thyme, 3 g (1/2 tsp) salt, and 1 g (1/2 tsp) black pepper.

Mix the olive oil, garlic, rosemary, thyme, salt, and pepper in a small bowl. Place the lamb chops in the air fryer basket and brush both sides with the olive oil mixture. Set the air fryer to 200C (400F) and cook for 10 minutes medium-rare or until the desired doneness is reached. Let the lamb chops rest for a couple of minutes before serving.

Lamb Shanks

Two lamb shanks, 30 ml (2 tbsp/1 oz) olive oil, 2 cloves (6 g) garlic - finely grated, 2 g (1 tsp) dried oregano, 2 g (1 tsp) ground cumin, 1 g (1/2 tsp) ground black pepper, 3 g (1 tsp) sea salt, 30 ml (2 tbsp/1 oz) lemon juice, 125 ml (1/2 cup/4 1/2 oz) white wine, 30 ml (2 tbsp/1 oz) tomato paste, 30 ml (2 tbsp/1 oz) honey.

Preheat the air fryer to 200C (400F). Rub lamb shanks with olive oil and garlic. Combine oregano, cumin, pepper, and salt in a small bowl. Sprinkle evenly over the shanks. Place lamb shanks in the air fryer basket and cook for 15 minutes. Whisk together the lemon juice, white wine, tomato paste, and honey in a medium bowl. Brush the mixture over the shanks and cook for an additional 15 minutes. Cook until the internal shank temperature is at least 63C (145F). Serve the lamb shanks with your favourite side dishes.

Meat & Potato Pie

250 g (9 oz) minced beef, 30 ml (2 tbsp/1 oz) oil, 1 onion - diced, 2 cloves (6 g) garlic - finely chopped, 2 g (1 tsp) smoked paprika, 2 g (1 tsp) dried oregano, 30 ml (2 tbsp/1 oz) tomato puree, 400 g (14 oz) potatoes - peeled and cut into chunks, 200 ml (7 oz) beef stock, 400 g (14 oz) puff pastry, 1 egg - beaten, and salt and pepper to taste.

Preheat your air fryer to 200C (400F). Heat the oil in a large frying pan and add the onion, garlic, paprika and oregano. Fry until the onion is soft. Add the minced beef and fry until it's browned, breaking it up with a wooden spoon. Add the tomato puree and cook for a few minutes. Add the potatoes and beef stock, season with salt and pepper and bring to a simmer. Roll out the puff pastry and cut out a slightly bigger lid than the top of your pie dish. Place the beef mixture into the dish and top with the lid. Crimp the edges to seal. Brush the top of the lid with the beaten egg and place the dish in the air fryer. Cook for 25 minutes until the pastry is golden and the filling is bubbling.

Meatballs

500 g (1 lb 1 oz) minced beef, 30 g (1/4 cup/1 oz) breadcrumbs, 30 g (1/4 cup/1 oz) grated parmesan cheese, 1 egg, 1 clove (3 g) garlic - finely grated, 2 g (1 tsp) dried basil, 3 g (1/2 tsp) salt, .5 g (1/4 tsp) black pepper, and olive oil spray.

Combine the minced beef, breadcrumbs, parmesan cheese, egg, garlic, basil, salt, and pepper in a large bowl. Mix well. Roll the mixture into 5 cm (1 inch) meatballs. Place the meatballs in the air fryer basket, making sure not to overcrowd them. Lightly spray the meatballs with olive oil. Set the air fryer to 200C (400F) and cook for 12-15 minutes until the meatballs are cooked.

Meatloaf

500 g (1 lb 1 oz) minced beef, 35 g (1/4 cup/1 1/2 oz) breadcrumbs, 60 ml (1/4 cup/2 oz) tomato sauce - ketchup, 25 g (1/4 cup/1 oz) diced onion, 1 egg, 2 g (1 tsp) garlic powder, and salt and pepper to taste.

Preheat your air fryer to 190C (375F). Mix the minced beef, breadcrumbs, ketchup, diced onion, egg, garlic powder, salt and pepper in a large bowl. Form the mixture into a loaf and place it in the air fryer. Cook for 15 minutes. Flip the meatloaf and cook for an additional 15 minutes.

Pork Chops

Four pork chops about 2.5 cm (1 inch) thick, 6 g (1 tsp) salt, 2 g (1 tsp) black pepper, 2 g (1 tsp) paprika, 2 g (1 tsp) garlic powder, 2 g (1 tsp) onion powder, 2 g (1 tsp) dried thyme, 2 g (1 tsp) dried rosemary, and 15 ml (1 tsp/1/2 oz) olive oil.

Mix salt, pepper, paprika, garlic powder, onion powder, thyme, and rosemary in a small bowl. Rub the seasoning mixture onto both sides of the pork chops. Place the pork chops in the air fryer basket and brush them with olive oil. Set the air fryer to 190C (375F) and cook for 15-18 minutes, or until the internal temperature of the pork reaches 63C (145F).

Pork Fillet

One pork fillet, 15 ml (1 tbsp/1 oz) olive oil, 2 g (1 tsp) garlic powder, 2 g (1 tsp) onion powder, 1.5 g (1 tsp) smoked paprika, 3 g (1/2 tsp) sea salt, and .5 g (1/4 tsp) black pepper.

Preheat your air fryer to 190C (375F). Mix garlic powder, onion powder, smoked paprika, sea salt, and black pepper in a small bowl. Rub the pork fillet with olive oil, then apply the seasoning mixture. Place the fillet in the air fryer. Cook for 5 minutes, then flip and cook for another 5-8 minutes or until the internal fillet temperature reaches 60C (145F). Allow meat to rest for 5 minutes before slicing and serving.

Pork Pie

500 g (1 lb 1 oz) minced pork, 140 g (5 oz) streaky bacon finely chopped, 30 ml (2 tbsp/1 oz) vegetable oil, 1 small finely chopped onion, 1 clove (3 g) finely chopped garlic, 2 g (1 tsp) dried sage, 2 g (1 tsp) dried thyme, 30 ml (2 tbsp/1 oz) Worcestershire sauce, 5 ml (1 tsp) English mustard, 250 g (8 1/2 oz) ready-made shortcrust pastry, and 1 beaten egg.

Preheat the air fryer to 200C (400F). Heat the oil in a large frying pan and add the onion and garlic. Cook for 5 minutes until softened. Add the minced pork, bacon, sage, thyme, Worcestershire sauce, and mustard. Cook until the mixture has browned and is cooked through. Set aside to cool. Roll out the pastry on a lightly floured surface and cut out two circles, one slightly larger. Place the larger pastry circle in the base of a greased pie dish and line it. Or use several small pie dishes. Fill with the cooled pork mixture and brush the edges of the pastry with beaten egg. Place the smaller pastry circle on top and press the edges with your fingers or fork to seal. Brush the top of the pie with the remaining egg. Place in the preheated air fryer and cook for 20 minutes until golden.

Pot Roast

1 kg (2 lb 2 oz) chuck roast or braising joint or shoulder), 60 ml (2 tbsp/1 oz) olive oil, 10 g (2 tsp) sea salt, 2 g (1 tsp) pepper, 1 g (1/2 tsp) garlic powder, 30 g (2 tbsp/1 oz), 1/2 onion - diced, 1 clove (3 g) finely grated garlic, 2 carrots - diced, 2 stalks celery - chopped, 125 ml (1/2 cup/4 1/2 oz) beef stock.

Preheat the air fryer to 200C (400F). Rub roast with olive oil, salt, pepper, and garlic powder. Place roast in a casserole dish, oven-proof bowl, or pan in the air fryer and cook for 25 minutes. Remove the roast joint from the casserole dish and set aside while adding butter, onion, garlic, carrots, and celery to the casserole dish and cook for 5 minutes, stirring occasionally. Add beef stock and stir to combine. Place the roast back in the casserole dish and cook for 15 minutes.

Roast Beef

1.4 kg (3 lb) roasting beef joint, 30 ml (2 tbsp/1 oz) canola oil, 2 g (1 tsp) garlic powder, 2 g (1/2 tsp) smoked paprika, 5 ml (1 tsp) Worcestershire sauce, and salt and pepper to taste.

In a large bowl, combine the oil and all the seasonings. Place the joint in the air fryer and brush the oil and seasoning mixture onto the beef. Cook the meat at 375F (190C) for 20 minutes per 500 g (1 lb 1 oz). After 20 minutes, turn the joint over and cook until the internal joint temperature reaches 63C (145F). Let rest for 10 minutes before slicing to serve.

Roast Pork

1 kg (2 lb 2 oz) boneless pork shoulder with a layer of fat and skin for crackling, 30 ml (2 tbsp/1 oz) olive oil, 4 g (2 tsp) garlic powder, 2 g (1 tsp) smoked paprika, 2 g (1 tsp) ground cumin, 2 g (1 tsp) onion powder, 1 g (1 tsp) dried oregano, 5 g (1 tsp) sea salt, and 1 g (1/2 tsp) black pepper.

Preheat the air fryer to 200C (400F). Combine the garlic powder, smoked paprika, cumin, onion powder, oregano, salt, and black pepper in a small bowl. Deeply score the skin, rub the pork shoulder with olive oil, and then season it with the spice mix. Place the pork shoulder in the air fryer basket and cook for 35-45 minutes until cooked. Let the pork rest for 5 minutes.

Rolled Brisket

1.5 kg (3 lb) boned, rolled, and tied brisket, 30 ml (2 tbsp/1 oz) olive oil, 4 g (2 tsp) smoked paprika, 2 g (1 tsp) garlic powder, 2 g (1 tsp) onion powder, 2 g (1 tsp) ground black pepper, 5 g (1 tsp) sea salt, and 30 ml (2 tbsp/1 oz) tomato paste.

Preheat your air fryer to 180C (350F). Rub the brisket with olive oil and seasonings. Place the brisket in the air fryer basket. Cook for 45 minutes. Remove the brisket from the air fryer and brush it with the tomato paste. Return the brisket to the air fryer and cook for 15 minutes. Allow the brisket to rest for 10 minutes before slicing.

Salisbury Steak

500 g (1 lb 1 oz) minced beef, 25 g (1/4 cup/1 oz) breadcrumbs, 35 g (1/4 cup/1 oz) grated Parmesan cheese, 1 egg, 5 ml (1 tsp) Worcestershire sauce, 2 g (1 tsp) garlic powder, 2 g (1 tsp) onion powder, 3 g (1/2 tsp) salt, .5 g (1/4 tsp) black pepper, 30 g (1/4 cup/1 oz) plain flour, 60 g (1/4 cup/2 oz) olive oil, 250 ml (1 cup/9 oz) beef stock, 6 g (1 tbsp) cornflour, and 15 ml (1 tbsp/1/2 oz) water.

Mix the minced beef, breadcrumbs, Parmesan cheese, egg, Worcestershire sauce, garlic powder, onion powder, salt, and black pepper in a large bowl. Shape the mixture into four oval-shaped patties. Place flour in a dish and coat each patty with flour. Heat the oil in the air fryer at 200C (400F) in a baking dish for 3 minutes. Place the patties in the oil and cook for 8-10 minutes per side or until they reach an internal temperature of 71C (160F). Mix the cornflour and water in a small bowl to make a slurry. In a saucepan, bring the beef stock to a boil. Stir in the slurry and continue to stir until the mixture thickens. Serve patties with gravy.

Shepherd's Pie

500 g (1 lb 1 oz) minced lamb, 1 onion - diced, 2 cloves (6 g) garlic - finely grated, 250 ml (1 cup/9 oz) lamb or beef stock, 120 g (1 cup/4 oz) frozen peas, 120 g (1 cup/4 oz) frozen corn, 30 ml (2 tbsp/1 oz) Worcestershire sauce, 2 g (1 tsp) dried thyme, salt and pepper to taste, and 960 g (4 cups/34 oz) mashed potatoes.

Preheat your air fryer to 200C (400F). In a large frying pan, brown the minced lamb over medium heat. Drain any excess fat. Add the diced onion and garlic to the frying pan and cook until softened. Stir in the stock, frozen peas, corn, Worcestershire sauce, and dried thyme—season with salt and pepper to taste. Bring the mixture to a simmer and cook for a few minutes until the sauce thickens. Spoon the meat mixture into a greased 20x20 cm (8x8 inch) baking dish or a fit for your air fryer. Spread the mashed potatoes on top of the mix. Place the dish in the air fryer for 20-25 minutes until the potatoes are golden.

Spam Fritter Balls

One tin of Spam - diced, 120 g (1 cup/4 1/2 oz) plain flour, 2 g (1 tsp) baking powder, 3 g (1/2 tsp) salt, .5 g (1/4 tsp) black pepper, 1 g (1/2 tsp) garlic powder, 1 g (1/2 tsp) onion powder, 1 egg, and 120 g (1/2 cup/4 oz) milk.

Whisk the flour, baking powder, salt, black pepper, garlic powder, and onion powder in a large mixing bowl. Add the egg and milk to the dry mixture and mix until a very thick batter forms. Mix in the diced Spam. Form the batter into small golf ball-sized rounds using a scoop or spoon. Place the fritters into the air fryer basket, ensuring they are not touching. Cook at 200C (400F) for 10-15 minutes or until they are golden brown and crispy.

Steak

One 226 g (8 oz) steak (sirloin, ribeye, or fillet), salt and pepper to taste, 5 ml (1 tsp) olive oil.

Rub salt and pepper into both sides of a room-temperature steak. Brush the steak with olive oil. Preheat the air fryer to 200C (400F). Place the steak in the air fryer basket and cook for 6-8 minutes for medium-rare, 8-10 minutes for medium, or 12-15 minutes for well done. Let the steak rest for a few minutes before slicing and serving. Note: Cooking times may vary depending on thickness.

Steak & Ale Pie

45 ml (3 tbsp/1 1/2 oz) vegetable oil, 1 onion, 340 g (12 oz) diced stewing steak, 30 g (2 tbsp/1 oz) plain flour, 350 ml (12 oz) ale, 30 ml (2 tbsp/2 oz) Worcestershire sauce, 45 ml (3 tbsp/1 1/2 oz) tomato puree, 2 g (1 tsp) dried thyme, 1 bay leaf, 140 g (5 oz) frozen puff pastry, 1 egg.

Heat the oil in a large saucepan over medium-high heat. Add onion and cook for 5 minutes or until softened. Add the steak and cook for 8 minutes or until browned. Sprinkle over the flour and cook for 1 minute. Add the ale, Worcestershire sauce, tomato puree, thyme, and bay leaf. Bring to a boil and reduce the heat to low. Simmer for 30 minutes or until the steak is tender and the sauce has thickened. Preheat the air fryer to 180C (350F). Grease a baking tray.

Roll out the pastry to .3 cm (1/8 inch) thick and cut out a circle slightly larger than the baking tray you will use. Place the pastry on the baking tray. Spoon the steak and ale mixture into the centre of the pastry. Brush the edges of the pastry with the beaten egg. Fold the edges of the pastry up and over the filling. Brush the top of the pastry with a beaten egg. Place the baking tray in the air fryer and cook for 15 minutes until the pastry is golden brown.

Toad In The Hole

30 ml (2 tbsp/1 oz) vegetable oil, 2 large eggs, 90 g (3/4 cup/3 oz) plain flour, 225 ml (3/4 cup/8 oz) milk, and 4 thick pork sausages.

Preheat your air fryer to 180C (350F). Add oil to a 20 cm (8-inch) round cake tin and place in the air fryer for 1 minute. Whisk together the eggs, flour and milk in a bowl until a thick batter is formed. Pour the batter into the cake tin and add the sausages. Cook in the air fryer for 15-18 minutes until golden and cooked. Serve with your favourite accompaniments.

Traditional Egg & Bacon Pie

You need enough ready-made shortcrust pastry for the top and lining of a 20 cm (8 inch) pie tin or quiche tin or one that will fit your air fryer, 8 rashers of lean bacon, 9 large eggs, 60 ml (4 tbsp/2 oz) skimmed milk, 4 g (2 tsp) chopped parsley, salt and pepper to taste, and 1 egg.

Fry or grill the bacon lightly to remove excess fat and remove any rinds. Place the partly cooked bacon on some kitchen roll for half an hour, then cut the bacon into pieces. Spam, bacon grill or luncheon meat can be great alternatives to bacon and should be prepared the same way. Line the tin with the pastry and evenly place the bacon or other meat. Gently mix 6 large eggs and the seasonings in a bowl or jug with the milk. Boil, peel and slice the other 3 large eggs. Gently stir the boiled sliced eggs into the egg, milk, and seasoning mixture, and slowly pour the mixture over the bacon or other meat in the tin. Place enough shortcrust pastry over the top and crimp the edges together after trimming any excess. Use a fork or knife for popping a few small holes in the top of the pie and brushing the surface with the small beaten egg. Cook in the air fryer for 20 minutes at 170C (340F). Rest for 5 minutes in the air fryer, then cook for 15-20 minutes or until the pastry is brown and the pie is cooked.

Beer Battered Sausage

For air fryer batter advice, see the Batter Splatter page.

Eight sausages of choice, 150 g (1 1/4 cup/5 1/2 oz) plain flour, 4 g (2 tsp) baking powder, 3 g (1/2 tsp) salt, .5 g (1/4 tsp) black pepper, 200 ml (3/4 cup/7 oz) beer, and oil for brushing.

Mix the flour, baking powder, salt, and pepper in a large bowl. Slowly pour in the beer, whisking continuously until the batter is smooth and has the consistency of heavy cream. Place the sausages in the batter, making sure they are fully coated. Place the sausages in the air fryer basket, brushing them with oil to prevent sticking. Set the air fryer to 180C (360F) and cook for 10-12 minutes, turning the sausages once or twice until the batter is golden brown and the sausages are fully cooked.

Baked Potato

Four large Russet potatoes, olive oil for rubbing onto the potatoes, salt and pepper to taste.

Start by scrubbing the potatoes to remove possible soil and pat them dry with a paper towel. Prick the potatoes with a fork to ensure even cooking. Rub the potatoes with a little oil and season with salt and pepper. Place the required potatoes in the air fryer basket and set the temperature to 200C (400F). Cook the potatoes for 30 minutes, flipping them halfway through the cooking time. Check the potatoes by piercing them with a fork.

Bannock

240 g (2 cups/8 1/2 oz) plain flour, 2 g (1 tsp) baking powder, 3 g (1/2 tsp) salt, 60 ml (1/4 cup/2 oz) warm water, 60 ml (1/4 cup/2 oz) milk, and 30 ml (2 tbsp/1 oz) vegetable oil.

Mix the flour, baking powder, and salt in a large bowl. In a separate bowl, mix the water, milk, and oil. Pour the liquid mixture into the dry mixture and stir until a dough forms. Knead the dough on a floured surface for about 1 minute. Shape the dough into a ball and place it in a cake tin in the air fryer. Set the air fryer to 190C (375F) and cook the Bannock for 10-12 minutes or until golden brown. Remove the Bannock from the air fryer and allow it to cool for a few minutes before slicing and serving.

Bread

385 g (3 cups/13 1/2 oz) of plain flour, 8 g (2 1/4 tsp) rapid-rise yeast, 9 g (1 1/2 tsp) salt, 8 g (1 tbsp) sugar, 240 ml (8 1/2 oz) water, and 30 ml (2 tbsp/1 oz) melted butter or ghee.

Mix the flour, sugar, salt and yeast in a mixing bowl. Gently add the water and melted butter. Mix with a spoon until there is no dry flour and you have a sticky dough. You do not have to knead the dough if you don't have time. Stretch and fold 3 or 4 times. Cover the dough with a clean towel and place it someplace warm to rise for an hour. Tip the dough onto a lightly floured worktop to a rectangular shape. Fold the top towards the middle, then the bottom over that, like folding a letter. Shape the dough into a ball shape (aka "boule") and dust with flour—place in a well-greased 18 cm (7 inch) cake tin. Cover with the cloth and leave to rise for half an hour. Preheat the air fryer to 200C (400F). Score the top of the bread with a knife. Brush the sides with melted butter. Place the tin with the dough inside the air fryer and cook for 10 minutes. Lower the heat to 180C (350F). Cook for 20 minutes. Remove the bread from the tin, place it in the air fryer basket, and cook for 5 minutes. Tap the underside to see if it sounds hollow and cooked. If not, cook it for another 5 minutes.

British Stuffing

60 g (2 tbsp/2 oz) butter, 30 ml (2 tbsp/1 oz) olive oil, 2 large onions - diced, 2 celery stalks - chopped, 3 cloves (9 g) grated garlic, 500 g (4 cups/1 lb 1 oz) cubed or crumbled day-old white bread, 1 g (1/2 tsp) dried thyme, 1 g (1/2 tsp) dried rosemary, 1 g (1/2 tsp) ground sage, 60 ml (1/4 cup/2 oz) chicken stock, 1.5 g (1/4 tsp) salt, and 1 g (1/2 tsp) ground black pepper.

Preheat your air fryer to 180C (350F). Melt the butter and olive oil over medium-high heat in a large frying pan. Add the onions, celery, and garlic. Cook until the vegetables are softened and fragrant, about 5 minutes. Transfer the cooked vegetables to a large bowl and add the cubed or crumbled bread, thyme, rosemary, sage, chicken stock, salt, and pepper. Mix well. Place the stuffing in the preheated air fryer basket or baking dish. Cook for 10 minutes or until the top is lightly golden brown.

Brussels Sprouts

500 g (1 lb 1 oz) Brussels sprouts, 30 ml (2 tbsp/1 oz) olive oil, 2 g (1 tsp) garlic powder, 6 g (1 tsp) salt, and 1 g (1/2 tsp) black pepper.

Preheat the air fryer to 190C (375F). Cut the larger Brussels sprouts into halves, leaving small ones whole and adding them to a large bowl. Drizzle olive oil on the Brussels sprouts and toss to coat. Add the garlic powder, salt, and black pepper and toss again. Add the Brussels sprouts to the air fryer and cook for 15 minutes, shaking the basket halfway through.

Bubble & Squeak

Two large potatoes - peeled and diced into 1.3 cm (1/2 inch) cubes, 1 large onion - chopped, 150 g (2 cups/5 1/2 oz) cooked shredded cabbage, 30 g (2 tbsp/1 oz) butter, 30 ml (2 tbsp/1 oz) vegetable oil, 6 g (1 tsp) salt, 1 g (1/2 tsp) black pepper, and 1 g (1/2 tsp) garlic powder.

Preheat your air fryer to 180C (350F). Place diced potatoes and chopped onion in a large bowl. Add melted butter and vegetable oil to the bowl and mix until potatoes and onions are coated. Add shredded cabbage to the bowl and mix until it is evenly distributed. Add salt, pepper, and garlic powder to the mixture and mix until evenly seasoned. Turn out the mixture evenly into burger patty shapes. Place the shapes in the air fryer basket and cook for 15 minutes. Turn them over and cook for 5 minutes until golden brown and crispy.

Cabbage

One head of green cabbage - cored and sliced, 15 ml (1 tbsp/1/2 oz) olive oil, 1 g (1/2 tsp) ground ginger, and salt and pepper to taste.

Preheat the air fryer to 190C (375F). Core and slice the cabbage and transfer to a bowl. Dispose of the core. Add olive oil, ground ginger, salt, and pepper, and toss the cabbage. Place cabbage in the air fryer basket and cook for 8-12 minutes, tossing the cabbage a few times during the cooking. Add strips of bacon or onion to the mix if you wish before cooking.

Cauliflower Cheese

One head of cauliflower cut into small florets, 30 ml (2 tbsp/1 oz) olive oil, salt and pepper to taste, 140 g (5 oz) grated cheddar cheese, 100 g (1/4 cup/3 oz) breadcrumbs, and 25 g (2 tbsp/1 oz) finely chopped fresh parsley (optional).

Preheat the air fryer to 200C (400F). In a large bowl, toss the cauliflower florets with olive oil, salt, and pepper. Transfer the cauliflower to the basket of the air fryer and cook for 12-15 minutes, flipping the florets once or twice until they are tender and lightly browned. Mix the grated cheddar cheese, breadcrumbs, and parsley separately. Once the cauliflower is cooked, remove the basket from the air fryer. Sprinkle the cheese mixture evenly over the top of the cauliflower, making sure to cover all the florets. Return the basket to the air fryer and cook for 3-5 minutes until the cheese is melted and bubbly.

Champ

Four medium potatoes peeled and cut into chunks, 1 large onion - chopped, 60 ml (1/4 cup/2 oz) milk, 30 g (2 tbsp/1 oz) butter, and salt and pepper to taste—chopped spring onion.

In a saucepan, boil the potatoes in salted water until they are soft, about 15-20 minutes. Drain and set aside. In a separate pan, sauté the onion in the butter until it is soft and translucent, about 5-7 minutes. Mash the potatoes with the sautéed onion, milk, salt, and pepper until smooth. Transfer the mixture to the air fryer in a heatproof dish and cook at 200C (400F) for 8-10 minutes or until heated through and slightly browned on top.

Cheesy Potatoes

Two large potatoes – peeled and cut into cubes, 15 ml (1 tbsp) olive oil, salt and pepper to taste, and 50 g (1/4 cup/2 oz) of shredded/grated cheddar cheese.

Preheat the air fryer to 190C (375F). Put the potato cubes into a bowl and toss them with olive oil, salt, and pepper. Place the potatoes into the air fryer basket in a single layer and cook for 15 minutes at 190C (375F), flipping halfway through. Next, place the potatoes in a heat-proof dish and cover with cheese. Cook for another 5 minutes until the cheese has melted.

Chickpea Meatballs

400 g (14 oz) tin of cooked chickpeas, 75 g (1/2 cup/2 1/2 oz) breadcrumbs, 40 g (1/4 cup/1 1/2 oz) grated Parmesan cheese, 15 g (1/4 cup/1/2 g) chopped parsley, 1 egg, 2 cloves (6 g) finely grated garlic, 3 g (1/2 tsp) salt, .5 g (1/4 tsp) ground black pepper, and spray oil.

Preheat your air fryer to 190C (375F). In a food processor, pulse the chickpeas until they are finely chopped. Mix chickpeas, breadcrumbs, Parmesan cheese, parsley, egg, garlic, salt, and black pepper in a large mixing bowl. Mix well. Shape the mixture into 2.5 cm (1 inch) balls. Spray the air fryer basket with cooking spray. Place the chickpea meatballs in the basket in a single layer, ensuring they do not touch. Cook the meatballs for 10-12 minutes or until golden brown and crispy outside. Serve the chickpea meatballs with your favourite dipping sauce or as a topping for salads or pasta dishes.

Chunky Chips

1 kg (2 lb 2 oz) Russet potatoes, 30 ml (2 tbsp/1 oz) olive oil.

Cut the potatoes into chunky chips or wedges and wash them in a colander under a cold tap to remove excess starch. Pat the chips dry with a kitchen roll. Place the chips in a large bowl. Add the olive oil and toss together to coat the chips. Add the chips to the air fryer basket and cook at 180C (350F) for 15 minutes, shaking the basket occasionally to cook the chips evenly. Next, turn up the temperature to 200C (400F) and cook for 15 minutes or until the chips are cooked and crispy or cooked to your liking, shaking the basket occasionally during cooking.

Crispy Fried Tofu

400 g (14 oz) of firm tofu - drained and pressed, 30 g (1/4 cup/1 oz) cornflour, 30 g (1/4 cup/1 oz) plain flour, 2 g (1 tsp) smoked paprika, 2 g (1 tsp) garlic powder, 2 g (1/2 tsp) salt, .5 g (1/4 tsp) black pepper, 60 ml (1/4 cup/2 oz) water, oil spray.

Cut the tofu into 1.3 cm (1/2 inch) thick slices. Mix the cornflour, flour, paprika, garlic powder, salt, and pepper in a shallow dish. Mix the water and a few spritzes of oil spray in a separate dish. Dip each tofu slice in the water mixture, then coat in the flour mixture, pressing the flour onto the tofu to adhere. Place the coated tofu slices in the air fryer basket, ensuring they are not overcrowded. Spray the top of the tofu with oil spray. Air fry at 200C (400F) for 15-20 minutes, flipping the tofu halfway through until golden brown and crispy.

Croutons

Four slices of bread cut into 1.3 cm (1/2 inch) cubes, 30 ml (2 tbsp/1 oz) olive oil, .5 g (1/4 tsp) garlic powder, .5 g (1/4 tsp) dried basil, and salt and pepper to taste.

Preheat the air fryer to 200C (400F) for 5 minutes., Add the bread cubes, olive oil, garlic powder, dried basil, salt, and pepper in a large bowl. Toss everything together to coat the bread evenly. Transfer the bread cubes to the air fryer basket in a single layer, ensuring the cubes are not overcrowded. Air fry the bread cubes for 8-10 minutes or until golden brown and crispy. Toss them a couple of times during cooking to ensure even cooking.

Fried Grated Potato

Two large russet potatoes - peeled and grated, 30 ml (2 tbsp/1 oz) olive oil, and salt and pepper.

Peel and grate the potatoes using a box grater or food processor. Place the grated potatoes in a clean dish towel and squeeze out as much liquid as possible. Mix the grated potatoes, olive oil, salt, and pepper in a bowl. Take small handfuls of mixture, press, and form each into your desired shape. Place them in the air fryer basket and cook 200C (400F) for 15-20 minutes or until golden brown and crispy.

Garlic Bread

Two cloves (6 g) of garlic - finely grated, 30 ml (2 tbsp/1 oz) butter - melted, 30 ml (2 tbsp/1 oz) olive oil, 6 g (1 tbsp) chopped fresh parsley, 3 g (1/2 tsp) salt, 1 g (1/2 tsp) black pepper, 4 hotdog buns or burger buns cut lengthways or across in half.

Preheat your air fryer to 200C (400F). Mix the garlic, melted butter, olive oil, parsley, salt and pepper in a medium bowl. Place the bun halves, outside down, in the air fryer basket. Brush the garlic butter mixture onto the halves. Place the basket in the air fryer and cook for 5 minutes until golden brown and crispy. Serve warm.

Garlic Mushrooms

500 g (1 lb 1 oz) mushrooms - sliced or whole, 4 cloves (12 g) - finely grated garlic, 30 ml (2 tbsp/1 oz) olive oil, salt and pepper to taste, 30 g (2 tbsp/1 oz) butter, 12 g (2 tbsp) chopped parsley.

Mix the sliced mushrooms, garlic, olive oil, salt and pepper in a bowl. Place the mixture in the air fryer basket or heatproof dish and cook at 180C (360F) for 12-15 minutes, occasionally stirring, until the mushrooms are tender and browned. Remove the mushrooms from the air fryer and place them in a serving dish. In a small saucepan, melt the butter over low heat. Pour the melted butter over the mushrooms and sprinkle with fresh parsley.

Garlic Roast Potatoes

Four to five medium-sized potatoes - peeled and cut into cubes, 3 cloves (9 g) garlic - finely grated, 30 ml (2 tbsp/1 oz) olive oil, and salt and pepper to taste.

Preheat the air fryer to 200C (400F). In a large bowl, toss the potato cubes with the garlic, olive oil, salt, and pepper until evenly coated. Place the cubes in the air fryer basket, making sure not to overcrowd them. Cook for 20-25 minutes, flipping halfway through and cooking until the potatoes are golden brown and tender.

Hasselback Potatoes

Two medium-sized floury potatoes, such as Maris Piper or King Edward, olive oil for drizzling, 1 rasher of uncooked bacon (optional), 1 onion-sliced, and salt and pepper to taste.

Start by preheating the air fryer to 180c (350F). Slice the potatoes into thin slices, leaving the bottom/underside intact. Place the potato in a greased bowl and drizzle with olive oil. If you wish, cut little pieces of bacon and onion and place them in the cuts to help keep them open and add extra flavour to the meal, but not so many pieces that the intense air fryer heat won't cook deep into the potato. Sprinkle with salt and pepper. Place the potato in the air fryer and cook for 15 minutes.

Marmite Roast Potatoes

Four medium-sized potatoes - peels on or off and chopped, 15 ml (1 tbsp/1/2 oz) cooking oil, 10 ml (2 tsp) Marmite, and salt and black pepper to taste.

Add the diced potatoes, oil, Marmite, salt, and pepper in a large bowl. Toss everything together until the potatoes are evenly coated. Preheat your air fryer to 200C (400F). Once the air fryer is heated, add the seasoned potatoes to the basket. Fry for 20-25 minutes, or until the potatoes are crispy and golden brown, flipping them halfway through cooking.

Mushrooms & Stilton

226 g (8 oz) sliced mushrooms, 120 g (4 oz) crumbled Stilton cheese, 30 ml (2 tbsp/1 oz) olive oil, and salt and pepper to taste.

Preheat the air fryer to 200C (400F). Toss the mushrooms with olive oil, salt, and pepper in a bowl. Place the mushrooms in the air fryer basket and cook for 10-12 minutes, until tender and browned. Remove the mushrooms from the air fryer and toss them with the crumbled stilton cheese. Return the mushrooms to the air fryer and cook for 2-3 minutes until the cheese is melted.

Potato Balls

400 g (2 cups/14 oz) mashed potatoes (floury potatoes like Maris Piper or King Edward), 50 g (1/2 cup/2 oz) grated Parmesan cheese, 30 g (1/4 cup/1 oz) flour, 2 eggs - beaten, and 30 g (1/4 cup/1 oz) fine breadcrumbs, salt and pepper to taste.

Mix the mashed potatoes, grated Parmesan cheese, flour, beaten eggs, breadcrumbs, salt, and pepper in a mixing bowl. Form the mixture into small balls. Preheat the air fryer to 200C (400F). Place the potato balls in the air fryer basket and cook for 6-8 minutes, flipping halfway through. Remove when they are golden and crispy.

Potato Cakes

Four large potatoes - peeled and grated 500 g (1 lb 1 oz), 30 g (2 tbsp/1 oz) plain flour, 20 g (2 tbsp/1 oz) grated parmesan, 30 g (2 tbsp/1 oz) finely chopped onion, 1 clove (3 g) garlic - finely grated, 20 g (2 tbsp/ 1 oz) parsley - chopped, 30 ml (2 tbsp/1 oz) olive oil, and salt and pepper to taste.

Preheat the air fryer to 190C (375F). Combine the grated potatoes, flour, parmesan, onion, garlic, parsley, olive oil, salt, and pepper in a large bowl. Mix until evenly combined. Shape the potato mixture into four patties. Place the potato patties into the air fryer and cook for 12-15 minutes, flipping the patties once halfway through. Remove and serve.

Potato Wedges

Four medium potatoes washed and cut into wedges with skins on, 30 ml (2 tbsp/1 oz) olive oil, 6 g (1 tsp) salt, 1 g (1/2 tsp) black pepper, and .5 g (1/4 tsp) garlic powder (optional).

In a large bowl, toss the potato wedges with olive oil, salt, black pepper, and garlic powder (if using). Preheat the air fryer to 200C (400F). Place the potato wedges in the air fryer basket in a single layer. Cook for 20-25 minutes, flipping halfway through until the wedges are crispy.

Ricotta Balls

150 g (1 cup/5 1/2 oz) ricotta cheese, 30 g (1/4 cup/1 oz) grated Parmesan, 30 g (1/4 cup/1 oz) plain flour, 1 egg, 2 g (1 tsp) Italian seasoning, salt and pepper to taste, 100 g (1 cup/3 1/2 oz) breadcrumbs, and oil spray.

Mix the ricotta cheese, Parmesan cheese, flour, egg, Italian seasoning, salt, and pepper well in a medium bowl. Use your hands to form the mixture into 2.5 cm (1 inch) balls. Place the breadcrumbs in a shallow dish and roll the balls in the breadcrumbs to coat them. Spray the air fryer basket with oil spray. Place the balls in the basket, making sure they are not touching. Set the air fryer to 200C (400F) and cook for 10 minutes or until golden brown.

Roast Courgette

Two medium courgettes cut lengthways into .7 cm (1/4 inch) thick slices, 30 ml (2 tbsp/1 oz) olive oil, 2 g (1 tsp) garlic powder, 3 g (1/2 tsp) sea salt, and .5 g (1/4 tsp) black pepper.

Preheat the air fryer to 200C (400F). Place the courgette slices in a bowl. Add the olive oil, garlic powder, sea salt, and black pepper. Toss until all slices are coated in the oil and spices. Place the slices in a single layer in the air fryer. Cook for 10 minutes, flipping the slices halfway through. Remove from the air fryer and serve.

Roast Potatoes

Four large potatoes peeled and cut into 4 cm (1 1/2-inch) chunks, 30 ml (2 tbsp/1 oz) olive oil, 2 g (1 tsp) garlic powder, 2 g (1 tsp) onion powder, 2 g (1 tsp) dried thyme, 2 g (1 tsp) dried oregano, 1 g (1/2 tsp) smoked paprika, and salt and pepper to taste.

Preheat the air fryer to 200C (400F). Combine the potatoes, olive oil, garlic powder, onion powder, thyme, oregano, smoked paprika, salt, and pepper in a large bowl. Toss until the potatoes are evenly coated. Place the potatoes in the air fryer basket, spreading them into an even layer. Cook for 20 minutes, shaking the basket halfway through.

Spicy Corn On The Cob

Four ears of corn without husk, 30 ml (2 tbsp/1 oz) extra-virgin olive oil, 1 g (1 tsp) chilli powder, 1 g (1/2 tsp) garlic powder, 1 g (1/2 tsp) cumin, 1 g (1/2 tsp) smoked paprika, salt and pepper to taste, 12 g (2 tbsp) freshly chopped coriander, and 12 g (2 tbsp) freshly grated Parmesan cheese.

Preheat your air fryer to 190C (375F). In a small bowl, combine the olive oil, chilli powder, garlic powder, cumin, and smoked paprika. Brush each ear of corn with the oil mixture, then season with salt and pepper. Place the corn in the air fryer basket and cook for 15 minutes, flipping the ears halfway through. Remove from the fryer and sprinkle it with coriander and Parmesan cheese.

Stuffed Mushrooms

Some of your favourite large mushrooms, grated cheese of choice, a little grated garlic, and some chopped fresh herbs of your liking.

Start by cleaning your mushrooms and removing the stems. Next, take a spoon and scoop out the inside of the mushrooms so that it forms a cup-like shape. Next, mix your cheese, garlic, and herbs in a bowl. Fill each mushroom cup with the mixture and place them in the air fryer. Cook for about 8 minutes at 200C (400F) or until the cheese has melted and is golden brown.

Sweet Potato Chips

Start by cutting the sweet potatoes into evenly sized chips. Next, toss the chips with oil and seasonings, such as salt and pepper. Next, place the chips in the air fryer basket in a single layer. Cook at 190C (375F) for 10 minutes, shake the basket and cook for 5-10 minutes or until golden brown and crispy.

Welsh Lavercakes

This recipe varies by region. 240 g (8 1/2 oz) Laverbread seaweed uncooked, 150 g (5 1/2 oz) rolled oats, 8 slices unsmoked streaky bacon, olive oil spray, 1 g (1/2 tsp) black pepper, and 15 g (2 tbsp/1/2 oz) plain flour.

Preheat the air fryer to 200C (400F). Place the Laverbread seaweed into a medium-sized mixing bowl. Add the rolled oats and black pepper and stir until thoroughly combined. Sprinkle the plain flour on a work surface to prevent any sticking. Shape the mixture into small patties 1.3 cm (1/2 inch) thick. Spray the air fryer basket and place in the cakes, and spray a little oil over each. Cook for 5 minutes before turning over and cooking for 5 minutes or until cooked through and crispy outside. Serve hot on their own or with a traditional Welsh breakfast.

Yorkshire Puddings

Two large eggs, 170 ml (2/3 cup/6 oz) milk, 90 g (2/3 cup/3 oz) plain flour, 1.5 g (1/4 tsp) salt, and 30 ml (2 tbsp/1 oz) vegetable oil.

Whisk together the eggs, milk, flour and salt in a bowl until a thick batter forms. Grease with the vegetable oil, 8 individual Yorkshire pudding moulds or muffin tins or depending on the size of your air fryer, you might have to do them in batches. Preheat the air fryer to 200C (400F) and place the moulds in the air fryer with just the oil inside to let them get hot. Carefully remove the moulds after about 5 minutes and carefully pour the batter evenly between them, filling each one about halfway. Place the moulds back into the air fryer and cook for 10 minutes until the puddings are golden brown and crispy.

Apple Crumble

500 g (4 cups/1 lb 1 oz) peeled and thinly sliced Granny Smith apples, 50 g (1/4 cup/2 oz) granulated sugar, 5 ml (1 tsp) lemon juice, .5 g (1/4 tsp) ground cinnamon, .5 g (1/4 tsp) ground nutmeg, .5 g (1/4 tsp) salt, 60 g (1/2 cup/2 oz) plain flour, 100 g (1/2 cup/3 1/2 oz) packed brown sugar, 50 g (1/2 cup/2 oz) rolled oats, and 120 g (1/2 cup/4 oz) cubed cold unsalted butter.

Mix the apples, granulated sugar, lemon juice, cinnamon, nutmeg, and salt in a large bowl. Mix the flour, brown sugar, oats, and butter in a separate bowl until crumbly. Place the apple mixture in a heat-proof dish. Sprinkle the crumbly mixture over the apples. Set the air fryer to 185C (360F) and cook for 18-20 minutes or until the apples are tender.

Apple Pie

Two pre-made refrigerated pie crusts, 480 g (4 cups/17 oz) diced apples, 50 g (1/4 cup/2 oz) granulated sugar, 15 g (2 tbsp/1/2 oz) plain flour, 4 g (2 tsp) ground cinnamon, 1 g (1/2 tsp) nutmeg, 28 g (2 tbsp/1 oz) butter - melted, and 50 g (1/4 cup/2 oz) brown sugar.

Preheat the air fryer to 180C (350F). Unroll one of the pie crusts and place it in the air fryer basket. Combine apples, granulated sugar, flour, cinnamon, and nutmeg in a medium bowl. Pour the apple mixture into the air fryer basket. Drizzle melted butter over the apple mixture. Sprinkle brown sugar over the top. Unroll the second pie crust and place it over the apple mixture. Pinch the edges of the top and bottom crusts together. Place in the air fryer and cook for 20 minutes. Allow cooling before serving.

Apple Turnovers

Two large apples - peeled - cored - thinly sliced, 30 ml (2 tbsp/1 oz) melted butter, 25 g (2 tbsp/1 oz) brown sugar, 4 g (2 tsp) ground cinnamon, 30 g (2 tbsp/1 oz) cornflour, 1 g (1/2 tsp) ground nutmeg, 15 ml (1 tbsp/1/2 oz) lemon juice, 2 sheets of thawed puff pastry, 1 beaten egg.

Preheat the air fryer to 180C (350F). Combine the sliced apples, butter, brown sugar, cinnamon, cornflour, nutmeg, and lemon juice in a medium-sized bowl. Mix until all of the ingredients are combined. Cut puff pastry into four equal-sized squares. Place the apple mixture in the centre of each pastry square, then fold the pastry over to make a triangle or square, depending on the size of the puff pastry sheets. Use a fork to press down the edges. Place the turnovers in the air fryer basket. Brush the tops of the turnovers with the beaten egg. Cook for 12-15 minutes or until the pastry is golden brown and the apples are tender.

Baked Oatmeal

220 g (2 cups/8 oz) of old-fashioned oats, 500 ml (2 cups/17 1/2 oz) milk of your choice, 60 ml (1/4 cup/2 oz) maple syrup, 2 g (1 tsp) ground cinnamon, 30 g (2 tbsp/1 oz) melted butter, 10 ml (2 tsp) vanilla extract, 3 g (1/2 tsp) salt, and 90 g (1/2 cup/3 oz) dried fruit of your choice.

Preheat your air fryer to 180C (350F). In a medium bowl, stir the oats, milk, maple syrup, cinnamon, butter, vanilla extract, and salt until combined. Stir in the dried fruit. Grease the air fryer basket with cooking spray. Pour the oat mixture into the air fryer basket. Cook for 15 minutes, stirring halfway through.

Banana Bread

240 g (2 cups/8 1/2 oz) plain flour, 4 g (1 tsp) baking powder, 4 g (1 tsp) baking soda, 3 g (1/2 tsp) salt, 3 bananas - mashed, 120 g (1/2 cup/4 1/2 oz) butter - melted, 5 ml (1 tsp) vanilla extract, 90 g (1/2 cup/3 oz) brown sugar, 100 g (1/2 cup/3 1/2 oz) granulated sugar, 2 eggs.

Preheat your air fryer to 180C (350F). Whisk together the flour, baking powder, baking soda, and salt in a medium bowl. Combine the mashed bananas, melted butter, vanilla extract, light brown sugar, granulated sugar, and eggs in a large bowl. Add the dry ingredients to the wet ingredients and mix until just combined. Grease a standard loaf pan with butter or cooking spray and pour the batter into it. Place the pan into the air fryer and cook for about 30 minutes until a toothpick inserted into the centre comes clean. Let cool before serving.

Banana Fritters

Two bananas - sliced, 60 g (1/2 cup/2 oz) plain flour, 25 g (1 tbsp/1 oz) sugar, 1 g (1/2 tsp) baking powder, 1 g (1/2 tsp) ground cinnamon, 60 ml (1/4 cup/2 oz) milk, 30 ml (2 tbsp/1 oz) melted butter, and vegetable oil for frying.

Mix the flour, sugar, baking powder, and cinnamon in a medium bowl. In a separate bowl, whisk together the milk and butter. Add the wet ingredients to the dry ingredients and mix until just combined. Heat the oil in a tray in the air fryer to 175C (350F). Dip the banana slices in the batter and carefully place them in the air fryer. Cook for 5 minutes or until golden brown.

Beer Battered Mars Bars

For air fryer batter advice, see the Batter Splatter page.

125 ml (1/2 cup/4 1/2 oz) beer, 80 g (3/4 cup/3 oz) plain flour, 2 g (1 tsp) baking powder, 3 g (1/2 tsp) salt, 2 to 4 Mars Bars, and oil spray.

Preheat your air fryer to 180C (350F). Mix the beer, flour, baking powder, and salt in a bowl until a smooth batter forms. Cut Mars Bar in half or leave them whole. Dip each piece into the batter, then place them in the air fryer basket. Spray the pieces with oil. Cook for 8-10 minutes until the batter is golden brown.

Bread Pudding

500 g (5 cups/1 lb 1 oz) cubed stale bread, 500 ml (2 cups/17 oz) milk, 2 large eggs, 90 g (1/2 cup/3 oz) white or brown sugar, 30 ml (2 tbsp/1 oz) melted butter, 5 ml (1 tsp) vanilla extract, and 2 g (1/2 tsp) ground cinnamon. Add 90 g (3 oz) of dried fruit of your choice.

Preheat the air fryer to 160C (320F). Place bread cubes in a large, greased, oven-proof bowl and add milk. Let sit for 10 minutes so that the bread can absorb the milk. Whisk together eggs, sugar, melted butter, vanilla extract, dried fruits, and cinnamon in a separate bowl. Pour the egg mixture over the bread cubes and mix until evenly combined. Transfer the bread pudding mixture bowl into the air fryer basket and cook for 20 minutes, stirring every 5 minutes. Stop stirring and leave to cook for a further 5-10 minutes.

Cheesecake

150 g (1 cup/5 1/2 oz) Graham cracker crumbs or crushed digestive biscuits, 75 g (3 tbsp/2 oz) granulated sugar, 60 ml (1/4 cup/2 oz) unsalted melted butter, 680 g (24 oz) cream cheese - softened, 200 g (1 cup/7 oz) granulated sugar, 3 large eggs, 5 ml (1 tsp) vanilla extract, and 60 ml (1/4 cup/2 oz) soured cream.

Mix the graham cracker crumbs or crushed digestive biscuits in a small bowl with the sugar and the melted butter. Press the mixture into a 23 cm (9-inch) springform pan/false-bottom cake tray. In a large mixing bowl, beat the cream cheese and the cup of sugar until smooth. Mix in the eggs, one at a time, followed by the vanilla extract and sour cream. Pour the mixture over the crust in the cake tray. Place the tray in the air fryer and cook at 160C (320F) for 20-25 minutes until the edges are set and the centre is slightly jiggly. Turn off the air fryer and let the cheesecake cool in the air fryer for 30 minutes.

Chocolate Chip Biscuits

240 g (2 cups/8 1/2 oz) plain flour, 2 g (1 tsp) baking soda, 3 g (1/2 tsp) salt, 240 g (1 cup/8 1/2 oz) unsalted butter at room temperature, 150 g (3/4 cup/5 1/2 oz) granulated sugar, 140 g (3/4 cup/5 oz) brown sugar, 2 large eggs, 10 ml (2 tsp) vanilla extract, and 280 g (2 cups/10 oz) semisweet chocolate chips.

Mix the flour, baking soda, and salt in a medium bowl. Set aside. Beat the butter, granulated, and brown sugar in a large bowl until creamy. Add the eggs and vanilla and mix until well combined. Gradually add the flour mixture to the butter mixture until just combined. Stir in the chocolate chips. Form the dough into balls of about 30 g (2 tbsp/1 oz) each and place on a plate or baking sheet. Cover with cling film and refrigerate for at least 30 minutes or until firm. Preheat your air fryer to 180C (350F). Place the dough balls in the air fryer basket, ensuring they are not touching. Cook the biscuits in batches for 8-10 minutes or until golden brown.

Doughnuts

120 g (1 cup/4 oz) plain flour, 3 g (1/2 tsp) baking powder, 1.5 g (1/4 tsp) salt, 50 g (1/4 cup/2 oz) granulated sugar, 1 large egg, 60 ml (1/4 cup/2 oz) milk, 30 g (2 tbsp/1/2 oz) melted butter and 5 ml (1 tsp) vanilla extract.

Doughnuts are a European favourite loved by Britons. First, whisk together the flour, baking powder, salt, and sugar in a medium-sized bowl. Next, mix the egg, milk, melted butter, and vanilla extract in a small bowl. Pour the wet ingredients into the dry ingredients and whisk until combined. Spoon the mixture into an air fryer-safe doughnut pan and smooth the tops. Alternatively, do not use a doughnut pan; make doughnut holes by forming the mixture into circles. Place in the air fryer and cook at 180C (370F) for 8-10 minutes or until brown.

Eccles Cakes

226 g (8 oz) self-raising flour, 85 g (3 oz) butter, 2 g (1 tsp) ground cinnamon, 24 g (2 tbsp) caster sugar, 30 ml (2 tbsp/1 oz) cold water, and 25 g (2 tbsp) currants.

Preheat your air fryer to 160C (320F). Rub the butter and flour together in a bowl until it looks like breadcrumbs, then gently add a little cold water until the dough forms and roll it out. Next, mix the cinnamon, caster sugar and currants in the bowl. Divide the dough into 8 equal parts and shape them into flat circles. Add the currants mixture into equal parts, spoon onto one of the dough circles, and cover with the other, folding over the edge underneath. Place them in the air fryer and cook for 10-15 minutes or until golden brown.

Flapjacks

240 ml (1 cup/8 oz) milk, 1 large egg, 30 g (2 tbsp/1 oz) unsalted butter - melted, 5 ml (1 tsp) vanilla extract, 180 g (1 1/2 cups/6 1/2 oz) plain flour, 25 g (2 tbsp/1 oz) granulated sugar, 15 g (1 tbsp/1/2 oz) baking powder, 3 g (1/2 tsp) salt, 1 g (1/2 tsp) ground cinnamon, 1 g (1/2 tsp) ground nutmeg, 85 g (1/2 cup/3 oz) rolled oats, and cooking spray.

Whisk together the milk, egg, melted butter, and vanilla extract in a large bowl. Mix the flour, sugar, baking powder, salt, cinnamon, nutmeg, and oats in a separate bowl. Gradually add the dry ingredients to the wet mixture, stirring until combined. Grease the air fryer basket with cooking spray. Spoon 60 ml (1/4 cup) of the batter per flapjack into the basket and space them out evenly. Cook in the air fryer at 190C (375F) for 8-10 minutes or until golden brown.

Fried Ice Cream Balls

For air fryer batter advice, see the Batter Splatter page.

160 g (2 cups/5 1/2 oz) of your favourite ice cream - slightly softened, 240 g (2 cups/8 1/2 oz) plain flour, 2 large eggs - beaten, and 150 g (2 cups/5 oz) crushed cereal such as Corn Flakes.

Mix the softened ice cream, flour, and beaten eggs in a medium-sized bowl until you have a thick batter. Place the crushed cereal on a plate. Scoop out a large spoon of the batter and roll it into a ball. Roll the ball in the crushed cereal until it's completely coated. Place the ball on a greased air fryer basket. Repeat with the remaining batter. Set the air fryer to 190C (375F) and cook for 4-7 minutes or until golden brown.

Fried Pineapple

One cup of pineapple chunks or a can of slices, 15 ml (1 tbsp/1/2 oz) olive oil, 15 g (1 tbsp/1/2 oz) light brown sugar, 2 g (1 tsp) ground cinnamon, and a pinch of salt.

Preheat the air fryer to 180C (350F). Place pineapple in a large bowl. Mix olive oil, light brown sugar, cinnamon, and salt in a small bowl. Pour the mixture over the pineapple and stir to combine. Skewer the chunks and place them in the air fryer basket. Cook for 10-12 minutes, stirring once halfway through.

Lemon Drizzle Cake

220 g (1 3/4 cups/8 oz) self-raising flour, 180 g (3/4 cup/6 oz) butter, 175 g (3/4 cup/6 oz) caster sugar, 3 eggs, zest of 1 lemon, 15 ml (1 tbsp/1/2 oz) lemon juice, 45 ml (3 tbsp/1 1/2 oz) milk. **For Drizzle:** 25 g (2 tbsp) caster sugar (granulated sugar works) and 30 ml (2 tbsp/1 oz) lemon juice.

Preheat your air fryer to 160C (320F). Cream the butter and sugar until light and fluffy in a medium bowl. Add in the eggs, one at a time, beating well after each addition. Add in the lemon zest and lemon juice, stirring to combine. Gradually add in the flour, stirring until a soft dough forms. Grease and line a 20 cm (8 inch) cake tin with parchment paper. Spoon the batter into the tin and bake in the air fryer for 25-30 minutes until golden brown and a skewer inserted into the centre comes out clean. **Drizzle:** Mix the sugar and lemon juice in a small bowl. Once the cake is cooked, remove it from the air fryer and brush the top with the drizzle.

Melting Moments

125 g (4 1/2 oz) unsalted butter - softened, 60 g (2 oz) caster sugar, 5 ml (1 tsp) vanilla extract, 175 g (6 oz) plain flour, 50 g (2 oz) cornflour, and a pinch of salt.

Cream the butter, vanilla, and sugar in a large bowl until light and fluffy. Sift in the flour, cornflour and salt and mix until a dough forms. Roll spoons of the mixture into balls and place them onto a plate. Cover and refrigerate for 30 minutes. Preheat your air fryer to 180C (350F). Place the dough balls into the air fryer basket in a single layer, ensuring they are not touching. Cook for 12-15 minutes or until lightly golden. Alternatively, place one on another with jam or cream between them or blob jam on the top.

Parkin

175 g (6 oz) self-raising flour, 120 g (4 oz) medium oatmeal, 120 g (4 oz) golden syrup, 120 g (4 oz) fat (lard/butter/margarine), 60 g (2 oz) demerara sugar, 2 g (1 tsp) ground ginger, and 1 g (1/2 tsp) ground cinnamon.

Preheat the air fryer to 180C (350F). Put the fat into a heatproof bowl, place it over a pan of simmering water, and let it melt. Remove the bowl from the heat and add the golden syrup, sugar, ginger, and cinnamon. Stir in the oatmeal and flour until well-mixed. Grease a 20 cm (8 inch) square cake tin or one that will fit your air fryer and spoon the mixture. Cook in the air fryer for 20 minutes until golden brown. Allow cooling before cutting into slices.

Peach Cobbler

30 ml (2 tbsp/1 oz) melted butter, 50 g (1/4 cup/2 oz) sugar, 15 g (2 tbsp/1/2 oz) plain flour, .5 g (1/4 tsp) ground cinnamon, .5 g (1/4 tsp) ground nutmeg, 300 g (2 cups/10 oz) sliced fresh peaches, 25 g (1/4 cup/1 oz) Scottish oats, and 25 g (2 tbsp/1 oz) brown sugar.

Preheat your air fryer to 190C (375F). Mix the melted butter, sugar, flour, cinnamon, and nutmeg in a medium bowl until combined. Add the sliced peaches and stir until everything is coated. Spread the mixture into a greased 18 cm (7 inch) round or square cake pan or ovenproof dish. Sprinkle the oats and brown sugar over the top. Place the pan in the air fryer and cook for 15-20 minutes. Let cool for at least 10 minutes before serving.

Rhubarb & Custard

Four stalks of fresh rhubarb cut into 5 cm (2-inch) pieces, 120 ml (1/2 cup/4 oz) custard, 15 g (1 tbsp) sugar, 2 g (1 tsp) cornflour, 1.25 ml (1/4 tsp) vanilla extract, and a pinch of salt.

Preheat your air fryer to 200C (400F). Mix the rhubarb pieces, sugar, cornflour, vanilla extract, and salt in a bowl. Place the mixture in a single layer in a heatproof dish. Air fry for 10-12 minutes or until the rhubarb is tender and the mixture is thick and bubbly. Remove from the air fryer and separate into dessert bowls. Pour over warm custard and serve.

Rock Cakes

225 g (8 oz) self-raising flour, 2 g (1 tsp) baking powder, 50 g (2 oz) caster sugar, 125 g (4 1/2 oz) unsalted butter - made into small cubes, 2 medium eggs, 100 g (3 1/2 oz) mixed dried fruit (raisins, currants, sultanas, candied peel, or dried fruits of choice), and 30 ml (2 tbsp) milk.

Preheat the air fryer to 180C (350F). Mix the flour, baking powder, and sugar in a large bowl. Add the butter to the bowl and use your fingers to rub the butter into the flour mixture until it resembles breadcrumbs. Stir in the mixed dried fruit. Mix the eggs and milk in a separate bowl, then pour into the dry mixture. Stir everything together to form a sticky dough. Spoon the mixture into the air fryer basket in rough shapes, leaving a little space between each cake. Cook in the air fryer for 15-20 minutes or until the cakes rise and become golden brown. Remove from the air fryer and transfer to a wire rack to cool.

Scone Slices

240 g (2 cups/8 1/2 oz) plain flour, 10 g (2 tsp) baking powder, 2.5 g (1/2 tsp) baking soda, 1.5 g (1/4 tsp) salt, 60 g (1/4 cup/2 oz) butter, cold and diced, 125 ml (1/2 cup/1/2 oz) buttermilk, 50 g (1/4 cup/2 oz) sugar, 5 ml (1 tsp) vanilla extract, and 50 g (1/4 cup/2 oz) of sultanas or other dried fruits.

Preheat the air fryer to 180C (350F), then in a medium bowl, whisk together the flour, baking powder, baking soda and salt. Cut in the butter with a pastry blender or fork until the mixture resembles coarse crumbs. Next, whisk together the buttermilk, sugar, and vanilla extract in a separate bowl. Finally, add the wet and dried fruits to the dry ingredients and mix until combined. Put the dough onto a lightly floured surface and knead until it comes together. Flatten the dough into a circle, cut it into 8 slices, and pat them flat on the top and bottom—place in the air fryer. Cook at 180C (350F) for 12-15 minutes or until golden brown.

Shortbread Biscuits

240 g (2 cups/8 1/2 oz) plain flour, 100 g (3/4 cup/3 1/2 oz) unsalted softened butter, 50 g (1/4 cup/2oz) sugar, 1.5 g (1/4 tsp) sea salt, and 28 g (2 tbsp/1 oz) turbinado or demerara sugar.

Mix the flour, butter, sugar, and salt in a medium-sized bowl. Knead the dough until it forms a ball, then flatten it into a disc. Cut the dough into 8 equal pieces and roll each piece into a ball. Place the dough balls on a parchment-lined baking sheet and flatten them to 1.3 cm (1/2 inch) thick. Sprinkle the turbinado or demerara sugar over each cookie. Place the baking sheet into the air fryer and cook at 180C (350F) for 8-10 minutes. Let cool on a wire rack.

Spotted Dick

225 g (8 oz) self-raising flour, 115 g (4 oz) suet, 115 g (4 oz) raisins, 3 g (1/2 tsp) salt, and 180 ml (3/4 cup/6 oz) water.

Mix flour, suet, raisins, and salt in a large bowl. Slowly add water and mix until the dough comes together and forms a ball. Shape the dough into a fat sausage about 18 cm (7 inches) long. Place the dough in the air fryer basket and cook at 180C (350F) for 20-25 minutes or until golden brown. Slice the spotted dick and serve with custard or cream.

Treacle Tart

One sheet of shop-bought puff pastry - thawed, 240 ml (1 cup/8 oz) golden syrup or treacle, 240 ml (1 cup/8 oz) heavy cream, 3 large eggs, 3 g (1 tsp) lemon zest, and 1.5 g (1/4 tsp) salt.

Preheat your air fryer to 180C (350F). Roll out the puff pastry on a lightly floured surface to a thickness of about .3 cm (1/8 inch). Use the pastry to line a 20 cm (8 inch) tart pan or one that fits your air fryer, pressing the edges to seal. Prick the bottom of the pastry with a fork. Whisk together the golden syrup, cream, eggs, lemon zest, and salt in a medium-sized mixing bowl. Pour the mixture into the pastry-lined tart pan. Place the tart in the air fryer and cook for 25-30 minutes until the pastry is golden brown and the filling is set.

Victoria Sponge

226 g (8 oz) self-raising flour, 226 g (8 oz) unsalted butter at room temperature, 226 g (8 oz) caster sugar, 4 large eggs, 4 g (2 tsp) baking powder, 5 ml (1 tsp) vanilla extract, a pinch of salt, and strawberry jam and thick whipped cream for the filling.

Preheat your air fryer to 180C (350F). Cream the butter and sugar until light and fluffy in a large mixing bowl. Beat in the eggs, one at a time, followed by the vanilla extract. Sift in the flour, baking powder, and salt and gently fold the mixture until well combined. Place the batter evenly in two greased and lined 20 cm (8 inch) round cake tins. Place the tins in the air fryer, either one at a time or on a trivet rack and cook for 20-25 minutes or until a skewer inserted into the centre of the cakes comes out clean. Allow the cakes to cool before spreading a layer of jam and whipped cream on one of the cakes, then sandwich the two cakes together—dust with powdered sugar.

Home Chef Books

The Woodfire Way - NINJA Electric BBQ Grill & Smoker for Beginners

- Complete with vibrant colour images.
- It is brimming with handy tips and tricks.
- UK metric measurements.
- Effortless cooking charts for various foods.
- Guidance on Woodfire maintenance and usage.
- Grid pages to incorporate your recipes.
- Flavourful seasonings, rubs, sauces, and marinades.
- Delicious outdoor BBQ recipes
- Ingredients available in the UK
- Lined pages to jot down notes.
- Jerky preparation guides and tantalising marinades.
- Glossy cover for effortless cleaning.

The recipes in this book, "Air Fryer UK Recipes - Ultimate UK Cookbook" can easily be created in "The Woodfire Way".

Instructions: To infuse your air-fried dishes with a smoky flavour, add your choice of pellets to the smoke box and select AIR FRY, followed by WOODFIRE FLAVOUR. Set the TEMP and TIME according to the recipe's recommendations. Press START/STOP to begin preheating. Once the ADD FOOD message appears, open the lid, place your ingredients in the supplied air fryer basket, and close the lid to commence cooking. Follow the on-screen prompts, check on your dish occasionally, and remove it from the Woodfire when cooked to your satisfaction. If you prefer not to smoke your food, skip adding pellets to the smoke box and refrain from pressing WOODFIRE FLAVOUR.

MY RECIPES

Available in 5 stunning hardcovers.

When you go to the trouble of recording your favourite recipes, you want to feel those recipes will remain at hand for a lifetime, and you might want to pass them down through the family. This is why we only produce this book in hardcover.

Printed in Great Britain
by Amazon